HOW TO THINK
MORE ABOUT SEX

Also by Alain de Botton

Essays in Love
How Proust Can Change Your Life
The Consolations of Philosophy
The Art of Travel
Status Anxiety
The Architecture of Happiness
The Pleasures and Sorrows of Work
A Week at the Airport: A Heathrow Diary
Religion for Atheists

HOW TO THINK MORE ABOUT SEX

Alain de Botton

PICADOR

New York

www.picadorusa.com
www.twitter.com/picadorusa • www.facebook.com/picadorusa
picadorbookroom.tumblr.com

Picador® is a U.S. registered trademark and is used by St. Martin's Press under license from Pan Books Limited.

For book club information, please visit www.facebook.com/picadorbookclub or e-mail marketing@picadorusa.com.

The photographic credits on pages 183–185 constitute an extension of this copyright page.

Design by seagulls.net

Library of Congress Cataloging-in-Publication Data

De Botton, Alain.
  How to think more about sex / Alain de Botton. — 1st U.S. ed.
    p. cm.
  ISBN 978-1-250-03065-8 (trade pbk.)
  ISBN 978-1-250-03066-5 (e-book)
  1. Sex. I. Title.
  HQ21.B795 2012
  306.7—dc23

                                        2012037100

Originally published in Great Britain by Macmillan, an imprint of Pan Macmillan

First U.S. Edition: January 2013

10 9 8 7 6 5 4 3 2 1

Contents

I. Introduction

I

It is rare to get through this life without feeling – generally with a degree of secret agony, perhaps at the end of a relationship, or as we lie in bed frustrated next to our partner, unable to go to sleep – that we are somehow a bit odd about sex. It is an area in which most of us have a painful impression, in our heart of hearts, that we are quite unusual. Despite being one of the most private of activities, sex is nonetheless surrounded by a range of powerful socially sanctioned ideas that codify how normal people are meant to feel about and deal with the matter.

In truth, however, few of us are remotely normal sexually. We are almost all haunted by guilt and neuroses, by phobias and disruptive desires, by indifference and disgust. None of us approaches sex as we are meant to, with the cheerful, sporting, non-obsessive, constant, well-adjusted outlook that we torture ourselves by believing that other people are endowed with. We are universally deviant – but only in relation to some highly distorted ideals of normality.

Given how common it is to be strange, it is regrettable how seldom the realities of sexual life make it into the public realm. Most of what we are sexually remains impossible to communicate with anyone whom we would want to think well of us. Men and women in love will instinctively hold back from sharing more than a fraction of their desires out of a fear, usually accurate, of generating intolerable disgust in their partners. We may find it easier to die without having had certain conversations.

The priority of a philosophical book about sex seems evident: not to teach us how to have more intense or more frequent sex, but rather to suggest how, through a shared language, we might begin to feel a little less painfully strange about the sex we are either longing to have or struggling to avoid.

2.

Whatever discomfort we do feel around sex is commonly aggravated by the idea that we belong to a liberated age – and ought by now, as a result, to be finding sex a straightforward and untroubling matter.

The standard narrative of our release from our shackles goes something like this: for thousands of years across the globe, due to a devilish combination of religious bigotry and pedantic social custom, people were afflicted by a gratuitous sense of confusion and guilt around sex. They thought their hands would fall off if they masturbated. They believed they might be burned in a vat of oil because they had ogled someone's ankle. They had no clue about erections or clitorises. They were ridiculous.

Then, sometime between the First World War and the launch of *Sputnik 1*, things changed for the better. Finally, people started wearing bikinis, admitted to masturbating, grew able to mention cunnilingus in social contexts, started to watch porn films and became deeply comfortable with a topic that had, almost unaccountably, been the source of needless neurotic frustration for most of human history. Being able to enter into sexual relations with confidence and joy became as common an expectation for the modern era as feeling trepidation and guilt had been for previous ages. Sex came to be perceived as a useful, refreshing and physically reviving pastime, a little like tennis – something that everyone should have as often as possible in order to relieve the stresses of modern life.

This narrative of enlightenment and progress, however flattering it may be to our powers of reason and our pagan sensibilities, conveniently skirts an unbudging fact: sex is not something that we can ever expect to feel easily liberated *from*. It was not by mere coincidence that sex so disturbed us for thousands of years: repressive religious dictates and social taboos grew out of aspects of our nature that cannot now just be wished away. We were bothered by sex because it is a fundamentally disruptive, overwhelming and demented force, strongly at odds with the majority of our ambitions and all but incapable of being discreetly integrated within civilized society.

Despite our best efforts to clean it of its peculiarities, sex will never be either simple or *nice* in the ways we might like it to be. It is not fundamentally democratic or kind; it is bound up with cruelty, transgression and the desire for subjugation and humiliation. It refuses to sit neatly on top of love, as it should. Tame it though we may try, sex has a recurring tendency to wreak havoc across our lives: it leads us to destroy our relationships, threatens our productivity and compels us to stay up too late in nightclubs talking to people whom we don't like but whose exposed midriffs we nevertheless strongly wish to touch. Sex remains in absurd, and perhaps irreconcilable, conflict with some of our highest commitments and values. Unsurprisingly, we have no option but to repress its demands most of the time. We should accept that sex is inherently rather weird instead of blaming ourselves for not responding in more normal ways to its confusing impulses.

This is not to say that we cannot take steps to grow wiser about sex. We should simply realize that we will never entirely surmount the difficulties it throws our way. Our best hope should be for a respectful accommodation with an anarchic and reckless power.

The most urgent problems we face with sex seldom have anything to do with technique. *Kama Sutra*, India, late eighteenth century.

3.

Sex manuals, ranging from the *Kama Sutra* to *The Joy of Sex*, have been united in locating the problems of sexuality in the physical sphere. Sex will go better – they variously assure us – when we master the lotus position, learn to use ice cubes creatively or apply proven techniques for attaining synchronized orgasm.

If we occasionally bristle at such manuals, it may be because – beneath their encouraging prose and helpful diagrams – they seem intolerably humiliating. They want us to take seriously the notion that sex is troublesome to us chiefly because we haven't tried postillionage or got the hang of the Karezza method. Yet these are adventures at the luxurious end of the spectrum of human sexuality and mock the sorts of challenges we are more normally faced with.

For the majority of us, the real cause for concern is not how to make sex even more enjoyable with a lover who is already keen to spend several hours on a divan with us trying out new positions, amid the smell of jasmine and the song of hummingbirds. Rather, we worry about how problematic sex has become with our long-term partner due to mutual resentments over childcare and finances; or about our addiction to internet pornography; or about the fact that we seem to crave sex only with people we don't love; or about whether, by having had an affair with someone at work, we have irretrievably broken our spouse's heart and trust.

4.

In the face of these problems and many more, we might question our expectations of how often we can rightly look forward to sex going well for us – and, contrary to the spirit of the age, might conclude that a handful of occasions in a lifetime may be a fair and natural limit to our ambitions. Great sex, like happiness more generally, may be the precious and sublime exception.

During our most fortunate encounters, it is rare for us to appreciate how privileged we are. It is only as we get older, and look back repeatedly and nostalgically to a few erotic episodes, that we start to realize with what stinginess nature extends her gifts to us – and therefore what an extraordinary and rare achievement of biology, psychology and timing satisfying sex really is.

For most of our lives, sex seems fated to remain steeped in longing and awkwardness. Whatever the manuals may promise, there are really no solutions to the majority of the dilemmas sex creates for us. A useful self-help book on this subject ought hence to focus on the management of pain rather than its outright elimination; we should hope to find a literary version of a hospice, not a hospital. Yet though we cannot expect books to dissolve away our problems, they can still provide opportunities for us to discharge our sadness and discover a communal confirmation of our woes. Books retain a role in offering us consoling reminders that we are not alone with the humiliating and peculiar difficulties imposed by our unavoidable possession of a sex drive.

II. The Pleasures of Sex

1. Eroticism and Loneliness

1.

Before considering the many problems that sex causes us, it is worth taking a detour to look at the opposite side of the coin: to ponder the question – not as obvious as it may seem – of why sex should, on rare occasions, be such a deeply pleasurable and rewarding activity.

In so far as our age is interested in this topic, it tends to put forward a single over-arching explanation derived from evolutionary biology. This discipline, which is ubiquitous in the modern world, informs us that human beings, like all other animals, are genetically programmed to reproduce themselves and need the pleasures of sex as a reward for undertaking the immense efforts of getting together and raising children with a partner.

According to evolutionary biology, what we find sexy is really just a reflection of something that will further the species. We may be drawn to intelligence, because this indicates a quality that is important in ensuring the survival of our young. We like to see people dancing well as this indicates a vigour that will come in handy when protecting the next generation. What society calls an 'attractive' person is ultimately someone whom the unconscious intuits will be good at fighting off infections and go into labour without complications.

This evolutionary–biological thesis clearly isn't wrong. It is, however, blunt, disconnected from our actual experiences of sex – and in the end a little boring. While it successfully explains why sex exists, it doesn't begin to shed light on our conscious motivations for wanting to sleep with particular people or on the range of pleasures we derive from doing so. Evolutionary biology may provide us with an overall motive for our actions, but it doesn't develop any reasons that we actually have in our own minds while we invite someone for dinner and later try to unbutton their jeans on the sofa – and on this basis, it doesn't provide us with a very satisfactory account of why sex should really matter to us as reflexive humans.

2.

In search of an explanation that we can more directly relate to, we might begin by focusing on a singular moment in the dating ritual, one whose recollection, even many years later, will almost always be accompanied by a unique sense of excitement: the first time we kissed, and thus physically and openly admitted our attraction to, a particular person.

It might have been inside a car after a long dinner during which we barely dared to eat, or in the corridor at the end of a party, or quite suddenly, before parting outside a train station, without any concern for the many commuters pressing past on all sides. We may not be the finest conversationalists, but when we are describing how we met and the run-up to our first kiss, we are rarely dull.

This first moment, which decisively shifts us from relative strangers to sexual intimates, thrills us because it marks an overcoming of loneliness. The pleasure we take is not rooted purely in stimulated nerve endings and the satisfaction of a biological drive; it also stems from the joy we feel at emerging, however briefly, from our isolation in a cold and anonymous world.

This isolation is something we all become acquainted with after the end of childhood. If we are lucky, we begin comfortably enough on this earth, in a state of close physical and emotional union with a devoted caregiver. We lie naked on her skin, we can hear her heartbeat, we can see the delight in her eyes as she watches us do nothing more accomplished than blow a saliva bubble – in other words, than merely exist. We can bang our spoon against the table and inspire uproarious laughter. Our fingers are tickled, and the fine hairs on our head are stroked, smelt and kissed. We don't even have to speak. Our needs are carefully interpreted; the breast is there whenever we want it.

Then gradually comes the fall. The nipple is taken away, and we are blithely induced to move on to rice and morsels of dry chicken. Our body either ceases to please or can no longer be so casually displayed. We grow ashamed of our particularities. Ever-expanding areas of our outer selves are forbidden to be touched by others. It begins with the genitals, then spreads to encompass the stomach, the back of the neck, the ears and the armpits, until all we are allowed to do is occasionally give someone a hug, shake hands or bestow or receive a peck on the cheek. The signs of others' satisfaction in our existence declines, and their enthusiasm begins to be linked to our performance. It is what we *do* rather than what we *are* that is now of interest to them. Our teachers, once so encouraging about our smudgy drawings of ladybirds and our scrawls depicting the flags of the world, seem to take pleasure only in our exam results. Well-meaning individuals brutally suggest that perhaps it is time for us to start earning some money of our own, and society is kind or unkind to us chiefly according to how successful we turn out to be at doing just that. We begin to have to monitor what we say and how we look. There are aspects of our appearance that revolt and terrify us and that we feel we have to hide from others by spending money on clothes and haircuts. We grow into clumsy, heavy-footed, shameful, anxious creatures. We become adults, definitively expelled from paradise.

But deep inside, we never quite forget the needs with which we were born: to be accepted as we are, without regard to our deeds; to be loved through the medium of our body; to be enclosed in another's arms; to occasion delight with the smell of our skin – all of these needs inspiring our relentless and passionately idealistic quest for someone to kiss and sleep with.

3.

Let us imagine some incremental steps in the story of a couple seducing each other for the first time – and in so doing analyse their pleasures in relation to this thesis about loneliness. Let us begin by picturing the couple in a cafe at eleven o'clock on a Saturday night in a large city, eating ice cream after seeing a film together.

There is doubtless a biological explanation for the sexual excitement this couple are feeling, connected to an unconscious narrative about reproduction and genetics, but the man and the woman are also turned on by the overcoming of the many barriers to intimacy that exist in normal life – and it is this dimension we can focus on to explain the greater part of the eroticism they will experience on their way to the bedroom.

The Kiss – Acceptance

Spoon in hand, the woman is describing a holiday she recently took to Spain with her sister. In Barcelona, she says, they visited a pavilion designed by Mies van der Rohe and ate in a restaurant that specialized in seafood with a

Moroccan influence. The man can feel her leg beside his, and more specifically the elasticity of her black tights as they taper to the hem of her grey and yellow skirt. When she is in the midst of relating an anecdote about Gaudí, he moves his face towards hers, ready to pull back if she gives any indication of fear or disgust – but his advance is met, to his enchantment, by only a tender and welcoming smile. The woman shuts her eyes, and both parties register the unique, unexpected combination of moisture and skin across their lips.

The pleasure of the moment can be understood only by considering its wider context: the overwhelming indifference against which any kiss is set. It goes almost without saying that the majority of people we encounter will be not merely uninterested in having sex with us but positively revolted by the idea. We have no choice but to keep a minimum of sixty or, even better, ninety centimetres' distance between us and them at all times, to make it absolutely clear that our compromised selves have no intention of intruding into their personal spheres.

Then comes the kiss. The deeply private realm of the mouth – that dark, moist cavity that no one else but our dentist usually enters, where our tongue reigns supreme over a microcosm as silent and unknown as the belly of a whale – now prepares to open itself up to another. The tongue, which has had no expectation of ever meeting a compatriot, gingerly approaches a fellow member of its species, advancing with something of the reserve and curiosity exhibited by a South Sea Islander in greeting the arrival of the first European adventurer. Indentations and plateaus in the inner lining of the cheeks, hitherto thought of as solely personal, are revealed as having counterparts. The tongues engage each other in a tentative dance. One person can lick the other's teeth as if they were his or her own.

It could sound disgusting – and that's the point. Nothing is erotic that isn't also, with the wrong person, revolting, which is precisely what makes erotic moments so intense: at the precise juncture where disgust could be at its height, we find only welcome and permission. The privileged nature of the union between two people is sealed by an act that, with someone else, would have horrified them both.

Then again, if we lived in another culture where acceptance was signalled in other ways entirely – for example, where a couple who wanted to show one another signs of affection would eat a papaya together or touch each other's toenails – these actions might in turn also become eroticized. A kiss is pleasurable because of the sensory receptivity of our lips, but we shouldn't overlook that a good deal of our excitement has nothing to do with the physical dimension of the act: it stems from the simple realization that someone else likes us quite a lot, a message that would enchant us even if it were delivered via another medium. Beneath the kiss itself, it is its meaning that interests us – which is why the desire to kiss someone can be decisively reduced (as it may need to be, for instance, when two lovers are already married to other people) by a declaration of that desire – a confession which may in itself be so erotic as to render the actual kiss superfluous.

The Undressing – An End to Shame

The man and woman drive back to her flat in a part of town he doesn't know well and together climb silently up to the third floor. Inside, the curtains are open and the bedroom is illuminated by the orange light of a streetlamp. They kiss once more by a cupboard. Emboldened by their privacy, he undoes the clasps on her beige blouse, she unfastens the buttons of his blue shirt. Their movements grow impatient. He reaches around to her back and grapples awkwardly with the hooks on her bra. With a forgiving smile at his ineptitude, she reaches around to help him. A few moments later, they behold each other naked for the first time and begin tenderly caressing each other's thighs, buttocks, shoulders, stomachs and nipples.

It can hardly be coincidental that in Genesis, one of the principal punishments visited by God on Adam and Eve in their expulsion from Paradise was a sense of physical shame. The Judeo-Christian deity decreed that the two ingrates should forever feel embarrassed about exposing their bodies. Whatever we may make of the biblical origins of this feeling of corporeal shame, it is evident that we wear clothes not only to keep warm but also – and perhaps even primarily – for fear of provoking repulsion in others by the sight of our flesh. Our bodies never look quite as we would want them to; even in the most beguiling and athletic moments of our youth, we are rarely lacking a long list of features we would prefer to alter. Yet such anxiety is based on something more existential than a cosmetic distaste. There is something fundamentally embarrassing about revealing any kind of naked adult body – which is to say, any body capable of desiring and having sex – to a witness.

It wasn't always this way. The shame begins in adolescence. As our bodies mature and become physically ready for sex, so we run the risk of appearing obscene before the wrong eyes. A division begins between our ordinary public selves on the one hand and our sexual and private identities on the other. A large portion of who we are as adults, from our sexual fantasies to our parted legs, becomes impossible to share with almost anyone we know.

Let us return to our male lover, who is now passionately sucking his partner's fingers. For him, the division of selves and the feeling of infamy began in the middle of his fourteenth year. One month, he was happy to play cowboys and Indians in the garden with his brother and visit his beloved grandmother; the next, all he wanted was to stay at home in his room with the curtains drawn, masturbating to the memory of a woman's profile that he had glimpsed on the way out of the newsagent's. There was no way to reconcile his desires with what was expected of him by others. His era could coun-

During sex, we go (briefly) back the other way.
Masaccio, *Adam and Eve Banished from Paradise*, *c*.1427.

tenance his thinking of holding the hand of or even kissing a girl he liked, but such benign and innocent activities seemed to have little in common with the macabre depravity unfolding daily in his runaway imagination. Soon enough he was dreaming of orgies and anal sex, obsessing about obtaining hard-core pornography and fantasizing about tying up and defiling his maths teacher. How could he still be a nice person? His shame prompted him to develop an inner self that he feared he would never be able to introduce anyone to.

Something similar had happened to his partner, now on her knees before him. At thirteen, she too underwent a transformation. She had previously enjoyed needlework, horseback riding and baking banana bread. Then, all but overnight, her pastimes dwindled to one: going into the bathroom, locking the door, lying on the floor, pulling off her trousers and watching herself masturbate in the full-length mirror. How could such an activity fit in with what other people knew of her? Could anyone accept the whole of her? In the guilty, exhausted moments after reaching orgasm, she knew some of the pain felt by Masaccio's Eve as she was ushered out of Paradise by a punitive deity.

What is now unfolding between our couple in the bedroom is therefore an act of mutual reconciliation between two secret sexual selves, emerging at last from sinful solitude. The couple tacitly agree not to mention the stupefying strangeness of their respective physical forms and bodily desires; they accept without shame what once seemed so shameful. They admit through their caresses to being driven in unusual yet compatible directions. What they are up to is starkly at odds with the behaviour expected of them by the civilized world – it clashes, for instance, with the memory of their grandmothers – but it no longer seems either wicked or unique. At last, in the semi-darkness, the couple can confess to the many wondrous and demented things that having a body drives them to want.

Excitement – Authenticity

They lie down on the bed and caress each other further. He reaches down between her legs and presses gently upwards, realizing with intense joy that she is wet. At the same time, she stretches her hand across to him and takes comparable satisfaction in discovering the extreme stiffness of his penis.

The reason such physiological reactions are emotionally so satisfactory (which means, simultaneously, so erotic) is that they signal a kind of approval that lies utterly beyond rational manipulation. Erections and lubrication simply cannot be effected by willpower and are therefore particularly true and honest indices of interest. In a world in which fake enthusiasms are rife, in which it is often hard to tell whether people really like us or whether they are being kind to us merely out of a sense of duty, the wet vagina and the stiff penis function as unambiguous agents of sincerity.

So delightful are these involuntary reactions that, after making love, our couple will return to discussing them in relation to the earlier part of their evening in the cafe. He will ask her with a slightly mischievous look whether she was wet during her anecdote about going to Barcelona with her sister. And she will answer, with a smile, that yes, of course she was, the whole time, even from the moment they first sat down to order their drinks and ice creams. He will in turn confess that his penis was hard inside the folds of his trousers – producing a further round of mutual arousal at the thought that, beneath their sensible conversation, their bodies were already experiencing a desire radically in advance of their surface social interactions.

Moments when sex overwhelms our rational selves have a well-known habit of being erotic. A few weeks from now, our couple will go off to the seaside for the weekend. On the Saturday evening in their hotel, after a day of sunbathing and swimming, they will lie in bed together talking, and eventually the topic of sexual fantasies will come up. Both will admit that they rather like uniforms. He will tell her how much he loves the idea of a dignified and austere nurse wearing a sensible white overall; she will confide – flashing a teasing smile as she looks out of the window – that she occasionally feels turned on by men in elegant woollen suits, in particular the type of well-dressed young executives who look concentrated and stern as they walk across city streets, carrying their briefcases and copies of the *Financial Times*.

The eroticism of such uniforms stems from the gap between the rational control they symbolize and the unbridled sexual passion that can for a while, if only in fantasy, gain the upper hand over it. Most of the time, the people we come in contact with in daily life – from doctors and nurses to investment managers and tax accountants – aren't of course wet or hard while they talk to us; they haven't even noticed us properly and certainly are not about to interrupt a medical procedure or cancel a conference call for our sake. Their businesslike indifference can be painful and humiliating for us – hence the peculiar power of the fantasy that life could be turned upside down and its normal priorities reversed. In our sex games, we are able to rewrite the script: now the nurse wants to make love to us so desperately that she forgets she is there to take a blood sample; the capitalist, for once setting aside all consideration for money, sweeps the computers off the desk and begins a heedless kiss. As we have passionate sex in an imaginary stall in a hospital toilet or on the floor of an imagined stationery cupboard, intimacy – symbolically, at least – wins out over status and responsibility.

Many formal physical settings can be unexpectedly erotic in and of themselves. Just as uniforms can inspire lust by their evocation of rule-breaking, so too – and for similar reasons – it can be exciting to imagine sex in an unobserved corner of the university library, in a restaurant's cloakroom or in a train carriage. Our defiant transgression can give us a feeling of power that goes beyond the merely sexual. To have sex at the back of an airplane full of business travellers is to have a go at upending the usual hierarchy of things, introducing desire into an atmosphere in which cold-hearted discipline generally dominates over our personal wishes. At 35,000 feet up, just as in the office cubicle, the victory of intimacy seems sweeter, and our pleasure increases accordingly. We call the scenario in the plane bathroom 'sexy', but what we truly mean is that we are excited at having overcome an otherwise oppressive kind of alienation.

Eroticism is therefore seemingly most clearly manifest at the intersection between the formal and the intimate. It is as if we need to be reminded of convention in order properly to appreciate the wonder of being unguarded, or to keep crossing the border into the vulnerable self in order to sense with the right amplitude the special qualities of the place we have been allowed access to. This explains the appeal of memories of our first night with someone new, when that contrast was at its most vivid, but also, more sadly, the lack of eroticism we can feel at a nudist beach or with

A promising place to make love.

a long-term partner who has forgotten to guard his or her nakedness against the ever-present dangers of our predatory ingratitude.

Rudeness – Love

As they are making love, the woman manages to let the man know, in one of those subtle, almost wordless ways in which lovers sometimes communicate, that she would like for him to pull her hair. He feels tentative about it at first, it doesn't seem like a 'nice' thing to do, but it is evident that she is no longer interested in any standard definitions of that term. So he takes her chestnut strands in his hands and brutally pulls to the rhythm of their lovemaking. Encouraged by her enthusiasm, he then ventures to insult her, partly because he feels so tenderly towards her. With equal affection, and at a pitch of excitement, she accuses him of being a bastard, a monstrous and demeaning intruder. He holds on roughly to her shoulders. The next day, scratch marks will be visible across her back.

Normal life continually demands that we be polite. As a rule, we cannot win the respect or affection of anyone without severely repressing all that is ostensibly 'bad' within us: our aggression, our heedlessness, our impulse towards greed and our contempt. We cannot both be accepted by society and reveal the full spectrum of our minds and moods. Hence the erotic interest we feel (which is more accurately an emotional satisfaction) when sex permits our secret self to be witnessed – and then endorsed.

In the presence of someone who seems utterly assured of our virtuousness, we dare to share aspects of ourselves that we are otherwise frightened and ashamed of. We use words and gestures that would cause us to be labelled as maniacs in the world beyond. It can be a sign of love to be allowed to slap someone hard across the face or to clasp our hands forcefully around another's neck. Our partners thereby demonstrate to us that they know we are essentially honourable. It doesn't matter to them that we have darker sides; they can – like the ideal parent – see us whole and recognize us as being fundamentally good. We are granted an extraordinary opportunity to feel comfortable in our own skin when a willing and generous lover invites us to say or do the very worst things we can imagine.

When we are on the receiving end of this type of violence and rudeness, we may find a parallel pleasure, and a certain sense of strength, in being able to decide for ourselves just how insulted, hurt and dominated we are going to feel. We spend so much of our lives being maltreated by others in the ordinary world, we are so often forced to submit to the malevolent will of our superiors at a time of their choosing, that it can be truly liberating to turn the dynamics of power into our own theatrical performance, to subjugate ourselves voluntarily, in circumstances wholly of our own design and before someone who happens to be, at heart, both kind and good. We work through a fear of our fragility by being slapped and insulted at our command, enjoying the impression of resilience and empowerment afforded by encountering the worst that someone can think of inflicting on us – and surviving.

The bond of loyalty between a couple is apt to grow stronger with every increase in rudeness. The more horrifying we believe our behaviour would seem to the larger, judgemental society we normally live in, the more we feel as if we are building a paradise of mutual acceptance. Such rudeness makes no sense from an evolutionary–biological point of view; it is only through a psychological lens that being slapped, half strangled, tied to a bed and almost raped starts to feel like a proof of acceptance.

Sex temporarily liberates us from the punishing dichotomy, well known to every one of us since childhood, between dirty and clean. Lovemaking purifies us by engaging the most apparently polluted sides of our selves in its procedures and thereby anointing them as newly worthy. This is never more true than when we press our faces, the most public and respectable aspects of our selves, eagerly against our lovers' most private and 'contaminated' parts, kissing, sucking and thrusting our tongues inside them and thus symbolically lending our approval to their entire selves, much as a priest will accept a penitent, guilty of so many transgressions, back into the fold of the Catholic Church via a chaste kiss on the head.

Fetishism – Goodness

Our couple both have fetishes and as they make love, they take note of them and thread them into their gathering excitement. The word fetish is normally associated with extremity, even pathology, and certain pieces of clothing or physical features – like long nails, leather outfits, masks, chains and stockings. However, none of these appear on our couple's list of proclivities.

In a clinical sense, a fetish is defined as an ingredient, typically quite unusual in nature, which needs to be present in order for someone to achieve orgasm. The earliest, most well-known investigator of fetishes was the Austro-German doctor and sexologist, Richard von Krafft-Ebing, who in his book *Psychopathia Sexualis*, published in 1886, identified some 230 different kinds of fetishes, among these stigmatophilia (love of tattoos and piercings), dacryphilia (love of tears), podophilia (love of feet), sthenolagnia (love of muscles) and thilpsosis (love of being pinched).

The extremity of these examples can make it seem as if only the insane have fetishes, but this is of course far from the case. Fetishes do not have to be either extreme or incomprehensible. We are all fetishists of one sort or another, but for the most part rather mild ones who are well able to have sex without having recourse to our favoured objects. In this wider sense, fetishes are simply details – most often related either to a type of clothing or to a part of another's body – which evoke for us desirable sides of human nature. The precise origins of our enthusiasms may be obscure, but they can almost always be traced back to some meaningful aspect of our childhood: we will be drawn to specific things either because they recall appealing qualities of a beloved parental figure or else, conversely, because they somehow cancel out, or otherwise help us to escape, a memory of early humiliation or terror.

The task of understanding our own preferences in this regard should be recognized as an integral part of any project of self-knowledge or biography. What Freud said of dreams can likewise be said of sexual fetishes: they are a royal road into the unconscious.

The male half of our couple has a fetish for a particular style of shoe. At the start of their evening out, he noticed with considerable excitement that the woman was wearing a pair of flat, black, sensible loafers (of the sort often associated with librarians and schoolgirls, and in this instance manufactured by the Italian company Marni), and now, as they make love on her bed, though both are otherwise entirely naked, he asks if she might put them back on to enhance his pleasure.

To explain why the man delights in his partner's shoes, his whole past must be invoked. His mother was a successful actress who dressed in loud and immodest clothes; she especially loved leopard-skin prints, mauve nail polish and very high heels. Significantly, she also made it clear that she did not much like her son. She never praised him or showed him affection, instead giving all her attention to his older sister and to her various lovers. She didn't read her boy bedtime stories or knit winter jumpers for his teddy bears. Even now, as an adult, the man is secretly terrified of women who remind him of this self-involved and unsympathetic matriarch.

Although the man is not aware of it, his psychological history is the omnipresent filter through which he looks at shoes, and by extension at the women wearing them. Tonight's date, for example, could have taken a very different turn if his companion had arrived in a pair of Manolo Blahniks or Jimmy Choos: had the two of them ended up in bed at all, he might well have been impotent. But the loafers were, and are, perfect. They are a concentration of the qualities he is most anxious to find in a romantic partner. In two narrow assemblages of well-worked leather precisely twenty-two centimetres long, he detects the identity of his ideal woman: someone calm, endowed with good sense, restraint, decorum, modesty and a degree of

shyness to match his own. He is able to make love
to their owner, but if circumstances demanded or
permitted – if, say, she went away on a business
trip and he were left alone to house-sit for her – he
could also, and without difficulty, achieve orgasm
with the shoes themselves.

The woman, meanwhile, has a fetish of her
own. She loves the man's watch, of the old-
fashioned, second-hand kind with a well-worn
leather strap. She keeps her eye on it while they
make love; at one point she squeezes the man's
forearm between her legs and is thrilled by the
feel of the metal and glass against her skin. The
watch is of the same sort her father used to wear.
He was a kind, playful, brilliant doctor who died
when she was twelve, leaving an unfillable hole
in her heart, and all her adult life she has sought
out men who somehow summon up his particular aura and smell. The sight of the watch makes
her nipples harden because it sends a subliminal signal that her new lover may have important
qualities in common with the person she most
admired in the world.

Talking of things around wrists, the man has
another fetish in this area. He noticed after first
kissing the woman that she was wearing a rubber
band around her left-hand wrist. Krafft-Ebing

never got around to discussing this: there is as yet no recognized phenomenon called bandophilia – but this only shows how immature the field of fetishism still is and how much work remains for researchers still to do (also, how much work there still is for pornographers, because the fetishes that show up on porn sites and in films reflect a woefully narrow range of the sort of things that actually excite us. There are still so many websites to be built: to name only a few, sites for people turned on by cardigans, by blushing, by people driving and by people reading). The man likes the rubber band because it seems to have been placed there in a cheeky, casual, androgynous and robust gesture. It suggests someone who isn't bothered by the canons of high fashion, who feels inwardly free enough to dabble with an object of low perceived value. Once again, he is turned on by something that frees him from the shadow of his mother, who only ever wore jewellery from expensive shops (much of it bought for her on the side by men who were not his father).

An interesting, unexpected and surely unintended explanation for fetishes may be found in Socrates' famous dinner-party discussion about love, described in Plato's *Symposium*. Using Aristophanes as his mouthpiece, Plato articulates what has since become known as the theory of the Ladder of Love, which argues that whatever we are attracted to through our sense of sight leads us ultimately away from the merely visual, away from the material, and into a wider positive category referred to by Plato as 'the Good'. This construct of a ladder connecting the world of objects to that of ideas and virtues may usefully be co-opted to rescue our fetishes from the depressing alternative interpretation, which holds that they are trivial and inconsequential because merely sexual. Thanks to Plato's philosophy, a pair of beautiful loafers, a handsome vintage watch or an elastic band will no longer need to be dismissed as meaningless and incapable of producing anything more than unimportant and irrelevant pangs of desire. Rather, these and all our other fetishes may be

Objects turn us on as emblems of the Good.

seen as sitting at the foot of a ladder that climbs up to what we might love most in another human being. They turn us on because they are emblems of the Good.

Orgasm – Utopia

The orgasms that our representative couple end up enjoying in the early hours are, in sum, far more than just physical sensations generated by the friction and pressure of two sets of sexual organs obeying a biological command to propagate the species. The pleasure we derive from sex is also bound up with our recognizing, and giving a distinctive seal of approval to, those ingredients of a good life whose presence we have detected in another person. The more closely we analyse what we consider 'sexy', the more clearly we will understand that eroticism is the feeling of excitement we experience at finding another human being who shares our values and our sense of the meaning of existence.

The orgasm itself marks the supreme moment when our loneliness and alienation are momentarily overcome. Everything we have appreciated about our lover – the comments he has made, the shoes she is wearing, the mood expressed by his or her eyes or brow – all of these are combined into a concentrated distillation of pleasure that leaves each partner feeling uniquely tender towards and vulnerable with the other.

There are of course ways to have an orgasm that have very little to do with finding common purpose with another person, but these must be thought of as a greater or lesser betrayal of what sex should really be about. At the near end of the spectrum, this explains the hollow, lonely feeling that normally follows masturbation; at the far end, it justifies the outrage we feel on hearing about cases of bestiality, rape and paedophilia – activities where the pleasure one party takes in the other is appallingly lacking in mutuality.

4.

One of the difficulties of sex is that it doesn't – in the grander scheme of things – last terribly long. Even at its extreme, we are talking of an activity that might only rarely occupy two hours, or approximately the length of a Catholic Mass.

The mood thereafter will have a tendency to be subdued. Post-coital sadness often settles over a couple. One partner or both may have an impulse to fall asleep, to read the newspaper or to run away. The problem is typically not the sex itself so much as the contrast between its inherent tenderness, violence, energy and hedonism and the more mundane aspects of the rest of our lives, the eternal tedium, restraint, difficulty and coldness. Sex can throw the challenges we face into almost unbearably high relief. Moreover, with our libido spent, our recent transport may seem inhibitingly strange and disconnected from what we think of as our regular self and our normal concerns. We may strive ordinarily to be sensible, for example, but only a moment ago – can it really be? – we were desperate to flog our lover. Contented though we generally are to be living in a modern and democratic society, we have just now passed the better part of an evening acting out a desire to be a sadistic nobleman holding a damsel captive in a medieval dungeon.

Our culture encourages us to acknowledge very little of who we normally are in the act of sex. It seems as if it might be a purely physical process, without any psychological importance. But as we have seen, what happens in love-making is closely bound up with some of our most central ambitions. The act of sex plays out through the rubbing together of organs, but our excitement is no boorish physiological reaction; rather, it is an ecstasy we feel at encountering someone who may be able to put to rest certain of our greatest fears, and with whom we may hope to build a shared life based upon common values.

2. Can 'Sexiness' Be Profound?

I.

When we say that we like someone because he or she looks 'sexy', it can sound as if we were evaluating another human being by an insultingly superficial standard. Our culture is strict on this point: announcing that we approve of people on the sole basis of their appearance doesn't go down well in civilized circles. Before declaring a preference for a particular person, we are meant to get to know him or her gradually and via words; we are not supposed to fall in love (or lust) at first sight. It may even seem like a betrayal of others' humanity to judge them principally by their looks, which they cannot radically alter, rather than their character, which they (supposedly) can. We think of people as being made up of inner and outer selves, and we privilege the former over the latter.

Nevertheless, it is hard to deny that our physical envelopes play an alarmingly important part in our destinies and desires. The wish to sleep with certain people can arise in us long before we have had the chance to get to know them properly – before, that is, we have had any opportunity to sit down and have a discussion with them about their history, interests and feelings. We may immediately call them 'sexy', perhaps judging on the basis of nothing more than a photograph or a glimpse in the street, and imagine the pleasure we would take in going on holiday with them, for no more intellectually well founded a reason than that they *look nice*.

This is shocking, to be sure, but in a book about sex, hard to ignore. So before we dismiss all physical appeal as being meaningless, we should ask what it is that we are really saying when we declare that someone's looks are a 'turn-on'. What is it that we are drawn to *in* them? What is the attractive person attracting us *to*, precisely?

Here again, evolutionary biology offers powerful and seductive answers. By its logic, we are attracted to beauty for a simple and definitive reason: it is a promise of health. What we call a 'beautiful' person – or, if we're feeling more informal, a 'sexy' one – is in essence some-one with a strong immune system and ample physical stamina. We like such individuals (or as we may put it, they 'turn us on') because we surmise – through that intuitive faculty that nature has granted us to make snap decisions in complex, time-sensitive situations – that with them we would have an unusually good theo-retical chance of producing healthy and resilient children.

An impressive range of studies has shown that when random groups of people from around the world are presented with photographs of various male and female faces and asked to rank them in terms of their beauty, the results are surprisingly consistent across all social and cultural milieus. A consensus emerges about which sorts of faces we find most appealing. From these studies, evolutionary biologists have concluded that a 'sexy' person of either gender, far from being an unclassifiable abstraction, is in essence someone whose face is symmetrical (that is, the right and left sides match precisely) and whose features are balanced, proportionate and undistorted.

Sexiness, it appears, is *not* in the eye of the beholder: in one study, 97 per cent of respondents were keener to sleep with the (more symmetrical) woman on the right.

In the picture on the right, the man's face has the optimal amount of fat in relation to his height and weight; in the picture on the left, the same face has an excess of fat. What we call 'sexiness' is synony-mous with what biologists term 'health'.

2.

It can be rather disturbing to have someone else predict whom we are going to want to sleep with before we have even had a chance to form our own opinion. The evolutionary biologists' experiments feel like one of those magic tricks in which a conjuror blindfolds us and uncannily foretells which card we are going to pick out from among a well-shuffled pack. But unlike conjurors, evolutionary biologists have no truck with the supernatural; they maintain that there are reasoned scientific motives behind our preferences for certain faces. Symmetry and balance matter so much to us because their opposites – facial asymmetry and imbalance – are markers of diseases contracted either in the womb or in the early years of life, at a time when the greater part of the self is still being shaped. A foetus whose DNA has been corrupted by microbes or who has endured debilitating stresses during the first months of gestation will reveal these misfortunes in the arrangement of his or her features. Our looks are indicators of our genetic destiny.

It is hard to dispute the evolutionary–biological thesis that for an ancient segment of our brain, which is obsessed with survival, beauty is the ultimate hallmark of health. Evolutionary biology also seems correct in ascribing considerable importance even to the most minor aspects of facial appearance – arguing, for example, that a millimetre more or less across the bridge of our nose or between our eyebrows may have major implications for the way people respond to us. The discipline absolves physical attraction of the charge of being purely superficial. While conceding that we judge people by their appearance, it holds that appearances themselves are anything but trivial and indeed point towards some rather profound qualities. To be turned on by someone is to be fascinated by something important about them, sexual desire and the appreciation of beauty are linked to one of life's great projects: the production of children.

3.

After a time, however, the biological explanation for attraction starts to deflate and become a little depressing, for it seems to limit our sexual concern for other people to a single qualifying criterion: how healthy they happen to be.

It isn't that we don't care about this quality at all. It's simply that, given the breadth of requirements that a decent shared life imposes, our positive feelings about the appearance of a prospective mate must have to do with more than just his or her bodily well-being.

The French novelist Stendhal offers us a way out of this scientific cul-de-sac with the maxim 'Beauty is the promise of happiness'. This definition has the immediate advantage of stretching our understanding of why we might describe certain people as being beautiful. It goes far beyond mere good health: we bestow the word on individuals because we detect in their faces a range of inner traits that we intuit would be of some benefit in the establishment of a successful relationship. We might, for example, perceive in their features such virtues as determination, intelligence, trust, humility and a gently subversive sense of humour. If it is possible for us subconsciously to find evidence of strong resistance to disease in the shape of a nose, why might we not also discover an indicator of patience in the lips, or a cathartic inclination to laugh at life's absurdities in the brow?

4.

Just how much information our faces can convey becomes apparent when we study portraits by great painters depicting attractive people we don't know in the flesh. Consider, for example, the rendition by Ingres of a certain Madame Devaucay. The subject is patently good-looking – hence healthy, according to an evolutionary–biological interpretation. But if we wish to explain her charm with any degree of complexity, we will need to look for virtues beyond the reproductive fitness of her DNA. She intrigues us, and may even turn us on, because her face hints at a range of qualities besides health – qualities that (without making any claims to scientific accuracy) we might be able to put words to, and that we might welcome in a flesh-and-blood partner.

Something about Madame Devaucay's mouth and smile speaks of *worldly tolerance*. It is easy to believe that we could tell this mouth almost anything (how we hadn't paid our taxes or had done something bad in the French Revolution or had unusual sexual tastes), and its owner wouldn't hold us primly to account, wouldn't react with shock or moralizing or provincial censorship; she would know her fair share about how troubled

More than just mere 'good health': sexiness is also a promise of happiness. Jean-Auguste-Dominique Ingres, *Madame Antonia Devaucay de Nittis*, 1807.

our souls can get without losing their claim to a fundamental decency. Her nose seems a repository of a native *dignity*. It somehow indicates that she is privileged but not spoilt, acquainted with suffering yet keen to maintain her elegance in straitened circumstances. Meanwhile, her hairstyle suggests at once a *sense of discipline* and a touching *sensibleness*. She might have learnt how to do her hair like this at convent school, where she would doubtless have been one of the favourites of the kindly nuns. As for her eyes, they articulate a bewitching *boldness*: they would gaze straight at a brutal inquisitor and never look away. She would not back down from her beliefs or betray her friends out of expediency.

If we appreciate Madame Devaucay's beauty, it is surely not just because we assess her as being healthy, but also because we are moved by her entire character as it skilfully expresses itself to us via the features of her face.

Like many other outstanding examples of the genre, Ingres's portrait teaches us that appearance can be a bearer of authentic meaning. Portraiture is instructive precisely because so much of a subject really *is* right there on the surface. The outer, bodily self does not always have to be at odds with an inner, deeper persona lurking beneath the skin; the two can be integrated and coincident. Our wanting to sleep with certain people because we find them physically seductive doesn't hence have to mean that we are ignoring who they 'really are'. Rather, we may be aroused by, and feel eager to get closer to, an exciting kind of goodness – or, in Stendhal's formulation, a promise of happiness – that we have correctly discerned in their lips, skin, mouth and eyes.

5.

The psychological aspect of an impression of 'sexiness' is also evident in the context of clothing, especially women's high fashion. Turning once again to the evolutionary–biological point of view, we might draw an easy comparison between couture's presentation of its product and the mating displays of tropical birds. Just as the quality of the plumage of these birds can indicate the presence or absence of particular blood parasites and thereby swiftly communicate a message about health to a prospective mate, so can fashion seem, at least from a distance, to be narrowly focused on accentuating signs of biological fitness, especially as these are manifest in legs, hips, breasts and shoulders.

However, fashion would be a rather one-dimensional business if it spoke to us only of health. There wouldn't be such intriguing differences between the wares turned out by companies and designers such as Dolce & Gabbana and Donna Karan, or Céline and Marni, or Max Mara and Miu Miu. The foregrounding of health may be one part of the mission of fashion, but on a more ambitious level, this art form also provides women with clothes that support a range of views about what it means to be an interesting and desirable human being. In all their infinite permutations, clothes make statements about values, ethics and psychological dispositions, and we judge them to be either 'beautiful' or 'ugly' depending on whether we approve or disapprove of the messages they carry. To pronounce a certain outfit 'sexy' is not just to remark on the possibility that its wearer might be able to produce thriving children; it is also to acknowledge that we are turned on by the philosophy of existence it represents.

In a given season, we may look at any designer's collection and consider how we are being invited by it to think of virtue. Dior, for example,

Marni (left), Dolce & Gabbana (right). When we say that clothes are 'sexy', we don't just mean that their wearers appear healthy; we are implying that we like the way they look at the world.

may be urging us to remember the importance of such elements as craftsmanship, preindustrial society and feminine modesty; Donna Karan may be stressing the need for independence, professional competence and the excitements of urban life; and Marni may be making a case for quirkiness, calculated immaturity and left-wing politics.

Getting turned on is a process that engages the whole self. Our arousal is an endorsement of a range of surprisingly articulate suggestions as to how we might live.

3. Natalie or Scarlett?

1.

Even if we appreciate the complexity behind the concept of sexiness, we can still feel puzzled by the fact that different people are turned on by such different things. Why don't we all like the same faces or clothes? Why are our sexual tastes so varied?

Evolutionary biology confidently predicts that we will be drawn to people on the basis of their evident health, but it has not put forward any truly convincing theories about why we should prefer one specific healthy person over another.

2.

If we wish to account for our mysteriously personal sexual tastes, we might begin by first trying to understand our no-less-subjective tastes in art.

Art historians have long been at a loss to explain why people should have such strong preferences for one particular artist over another, even when both are acknowledged masters who have created works of great beauty. Why does one person love Mark Rothko, for instance, but have an instinctive fear of Caravaggio? Why does another recoil from Chagall but admire Dalí?

A highly suggestive answer to this conundrum can be found in an essay entitled 'Abstraction and Empathy', published in 1907 by a German art historian named Wilhelm Worringer. Worringer argued that we all grow up with something missing inside us. Our parents and our environment fail us in distinctive ways, and our characters hence take shape with certain areas of vulnerability and imbalance in them. And crucially, these deficits and flaws determine what is going to appeal to us and repel us in art.

Every work of art is imbued with a particular psychological and moral atmosphere: we may say that a given painting is either serene or restless, courageous or careful, modest or confident, masculine or feminine, bourgeois

What would we need to be frightened of, or lacking in, to call this 'beautiful'? Facade of the Church of Santa Prisca y San Sebastian, Taxco, Mexico.

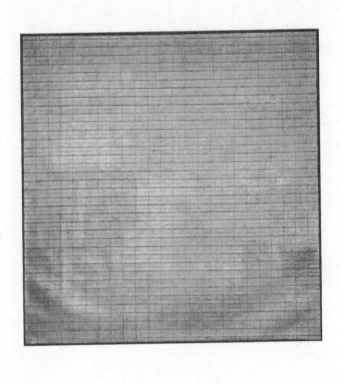

Agnes Martin, *Friendship*, 1963 (left); Michelangelo Caravaggio, *Judith Beheading Holofernes*, 1599 (above). Both are beautiful, but we have to be missing something quite particular in order to appreciate one or the other.

or aristocratic. Our preferences among these traits reflect our psychological histories – more specifically, what is vulnerable in us as a result of our upbringing. We hunger for artworks that contain elements that will compensate for our inner fragilities and help to return us to a healthy mean. We crave in art those qualities that are missing in our lives. We call a work 'beautiful' when it supplies the missing dose of our psychological virtues, and we dismiss as 'ugly' one that forces on us moods or motifs that we feel either threatened or already overwhelmed by.

3.

To flesh out his theory, Worringer proposed that people who are calm, cautious and rule-driven will often be drawn to a kind of art that is passionate and dramatic, and that can thus compensate for their feelings of desiccation and sterility. We can predict that they will be highly susceptible, for instance, to the intensity of Latin art, admiring the blood-red darkness of Goya's canvases and the phantasmagoric architectural forms of the Spanish baroque. But this same bold aesthetic, according to Worringer's thesis, will frighten and turn off other sorts of people whose backgrounds have made them anxious and overexcitable. These jumpy characters will want nothing to do with the baroque, locating far greater beauty in an art of calm and logic. Their preferences are more likely to run to the mathematical rigours of Bach's cantatas, the symmetry of formal French gardens and the quiet emptiness of canvases by minimalist artists such as Agnes Martin or Mark Rothko.

4.

Worringer's theory enables us to look at any work of art and ask ourselves what would have to be missing in someone's life in order for him or her to judge it 'beautiful', as well as what might be frightening to a person who would regard it as being 'ugly'. The very same approach can also provide fascinating insight into why we find some people sexy and others not.

As with art, so with sex: here too the accidents of nature and the quirks of our upbringing cause us to reach adult life in an unbalanced state, overly endowed in some areas and severely lacking in others, either too anxious or too calm, too assertive or too passive, too intellectual or too practical, too masculine or too feminine. We then declare people 'sexy' when we see in them evidence of compensatory qualities, and are repelled by those who seem prone to drive us further into our extremities.

Confronted by two individuals who are by appearances equally healthy – for the sake of this exercise, let's choose Natalie Portman and Scarlett Johansson – we may well feel, thanks to the unique mapping of our psychobiography, that only one of them is properly arousing in

Scarlett Johansson (left), Natalie Portman (right). Why aren't all healthy, attractive people equally appealing to us? Why do we have such pronounced individual preferences?

our eyes. If we were traumatized by overly theatrical and unreliable parents, we may decide that something about Scarlett's features suggests that she has just a little too much of a taste for excitement and melodrama. We may deem that her cheekbones indicate a capacity for self-involvement that we are already all too familiar with in ourselves, and that her eyes, though they seem at peace in the photograph we are studying, make her look too easily capable of exploding into just the sort of destructive rages to which we are in any case prone, and that we really don't need any help in bolstering.

We may end up favouring Natalie, who is objectively no more beautiful than Scarlett, because her eyes reflect just the sort of calm that we long for and never got enough of from our hypochondriacal mother. We may be turned on by the steely, practical resolve we detect in Ms. Portman's forehead, precisely because we cannot lay claim to the same trait ourselves (we're always losing the house keys and feeling confused about how to fill out insurance forms). And we may be seduced by her mouth because it implies a reserve and a stoicism that perfectly balance out our painful inclination towards brashness and intemperance.

In short, we can explain our relative attractions to Natalie or Scarlett by taking stock of what we are missing in ourselves, just as we can account for our preferences for the paintings of Agnes Martin or of Caravaggio by considering the different and particular ways in which we are deficient adults. We need both art and sex to make us whole, so it is not surprising if the mechanisms of compensation should be similar in each case. The specifics of what we find 'beautiful' and what we find 'sexy' are indications of what we most deeply crave in order to rebalance ourselves.

III. The Problems of Sex

1. Love and Sex

1.

Let's posit the following scenario: Tomas from Hamburg is on a business trip to Portland, Oregon, when he meets Jen. Both of them are 28 and in the computer industry. Tomas likes Jen immediately. As he gets to know her a little better over the course of a few days, he laughs at her jokes about people they both work with, admires her wry political analyses and intelligent opinions about music and films. He feels rather touched, as well, by a certain tender quality he detects in her: he thought it sweet when she told him, over dinner, that she still calls her mother every day even if she's travelling, and that her best friend is her little brother, who is eleven and loves to climb trees. When a friend asks Tomas about Jen, he confides that he finds her pretty cute.

She likes him too, but not in quite the same way. She wants to lie him down on the purple bedspread of her motel room (the Crown Court Inn) and straddle him. She wants to take him in her mouth and watch the look of pleasure on his face. Since they first met, she has fantasized repeatedly to the mental image of his semi-clad body arranged in various postures. Most recently, she imagined them doing it in one of the conference rooms they are using. But beyond his role in her sexual imagination, Jen – who is an honourable friend and a decent citizen and will one day be a good mother too – has no doubt whatsoever that Tomas would be an entirely inappropriate long-term partner for her. She can't picture herself enduring a lifetime's worth of his cheerfulness, fondness for animals and his enthusiasm for jogging. Last night, she had grave trouble concentrating on a long story he told about his grandmother, who is ailing in a care home with a disease which her doctors have been unable to put a name to. After sex, Jen would be more than happy never to see him again.

2.

The dilemma these two people face is endemic to our society, which even now offers us no easy way to articulate our frequently divergent desires for love and sex. We tend to tiptoe around what we want, cloaking our needs with evasions and in the process, we habitually lie, break others' hearts and suffer through evenings filled with frustration and guilt.

We have not reached a stage of human development in which Jen could openly tell Tomas that she wants only to have sex with him, and nothing more. To most ears, such an admission would sound rude (perhaps even cruel), animalistic and vulgar.

But then again, Tomas can't be honest about what *he* wants, either, because his longing to find love with Jen would seem soppy and weak. The taboo preventing him from announcing to her, 'I want to love you and look after you tenderly for the rest of my life,' is just as strong as the one that stops her saying to him, 'I'd like to fuck you in my motel room and then say goodbye to you for ever.'

To stand any chance of success, both parties have to lie about their desires. Jen has to take care not to let on that her interest in Tomas is purely sexual and Tomas cannot give voice to his own ambition for love, for fear that Jen might just as speedily make for the exit. Both hope that they may somehow manage to get what they want without ever having explicitly to specify what it is. Such ambiguity typically occasions only betrayals and shattered expectations. The person who wants love but gets just sex feels used. The person who is really after sex but who must pretend to want love in order to get it feels, if forced into a relationship, trapped or, if able to flee one, corrupt and dishonourable.

3.

How might our society enable Tomas and Jen, and others like them, to advance towards a better outcome? First, by recognizing that neither need has the moral advantage: wanting love more than sex, or even instead of it, isn't 'better' or 'worse' than the reverse. Both needs have their place in our human repertoire of feelings and desires. Second, as a society, we have to find ways to make sure that these two needs can be freely claimed, without fear of blame or moral condemnation. We have to mitigate the taboos surrounding both appetites, so as to minimize the necessity of dissimulation and thereby the heartbreak and guilt it causes.

So long as the only way to get sex is to feign being in love, some of us will lie and make a run for it. And so long as the only way to have a chance of finding long-term love is to hold ourselves out as devil-may-care adventurers ready to have no-strings-attached sex with near strangers in a motel, others of us are going to be at risk of feeling painfully abandoned the next morning.

It's time for the need for sex and the need for love to be granted equal standing, without an added moral gloss. Both may be independently felt and are of comparable value and validity. Both shouldn't require us to lie in order to claim them.

2. Sexual Rejection

I.

When we are told by someone we are attracted to, in that agonizingly sweet tone in which such news is generally delivered, that he or she would actually rather just be good friends with us, what we often hear is confirmation that we really are, as we have secretly suspected all along, a monstrous, ungainly, untouchable aberration – in short, a modern-day Elephant Man or Woman. Rejection hurts so much because we take it as a damning judgement passed not merely on our physical appeal but on our entire selves, and by extension (at this stage we're crying into our pillow, as something by Bach or Leonard Cohen plays on the stereo) on our very right to exist.

2.

An earlier section of this book argued with some vehemence that our apparently superficial sexual attraction to others can actually signal a much deeper understanding and appreciation of their inner self. Now we would do well to nuance that point, in the interests of retaining our sanity after a letdown.

We don't have to take sexual rejection as a sure indication that another person has looked into our soul and registered disgust at every aspect of our being. The reality is usually much simpler and less shattering than that: for whatever reason, this particular individual just can't get turned on by our body. We can take comfort in the knowledge that such a verdict is automatic, preconscious and immutable. The one doing the rejecting isn't being intentionally nasty; he or she has no choice. We can't decide whom we are going to be turned on by any more than we can will a certain flavour of ice cream or style of painting to be our favourite.

At moments of crisis, we have only to recall how we ourselves felt about people whom it might have been convenient for us to desire (because they were kind and available and liked us) but who nevertheless left us cold. We did not hate these unfortunates. We may have dearly wished we wanted to sleep with them, we may truly have thought them delightful, but our sexual compass had other ideas and could not be persuaded to alter its setting.

3.

At the heart of the pain created by sexual rejection is our habit of interpreting it as a *moral judgement,* when it might more accurately be categorized as a mere *accident.* We can start to break free from this torture by recognizing that the evenings that don't work out are really just a minor species of bad luck.

The history of weather helps to show us the way in this matter. In almost all primitive societies, people began by interpreting bad storms (which ruined crops and flooded settlements and dwellings) as punishments from above, signs that the gods were angry and human beings culpable. Gradually, the science of meteorology has helped to free our race from such inaccurate and pernicious superstitions. *We* are not to blame for the relentless rain, we now know; it's just the end result of a random interplay of atmospheric conditions over the ocean or behind the mountain range. Freakish bad luck, not something of our own doing, has caused our fields to be drenched and our bridges to be swept away like matchsticks by swollen brown waters. We'd be adding paranoia to misery to take the rain *personally*.

As we have learnt to regard the weather, so too should we understand those who tell us so sweetly that they feel like making an early night of it. We don't choose whom we want to sleep with; science and psychoanalysis have by now made it clear that there are hidden forces that make the choice for us long before our conscious mind can have any say in the matter.

However unbelievable it may seem when we are at the epicentre of suffering, sometimes a no is just a no.

3. Lack of Desire

i. Infrequency

1.

Let's picture a couple, Daisy and Jim. They have been married for seven years and have two small children, Mary (age 2) and William (age 6). At nine-thirty on a weeknight, in a bedroom in South London, they are reclining on their marriage bed, Daisy on one side, Jim on the other. The television is switched on to a travel programme about Italy and its cuisine, which Daisy is not paying much attention to, for she is occupied by plucking her eyebrows with the help of a pair of tweezers and a small mirror. The brows are vigorous in their growth, a feature that Jim admires and superstitiously interprets as a reflection of his wife's sexual energy.

Daisy had a shower a little while ago and is now lying loosely wrapped in a white towel that leaves her breasts exposed. Although during their early courtship Jim spent a great deal of time trying to imagine what these breasts might look like, and though he lost all command over his rational faculties on first encircling their areolae with his tongue, they now rest placidly before him without advancing a claim to be considered any more deserving of note, remark or excitement than, say, a thumb or a shin. Eroticism seems, in the end, to have very little to do with simply being unclothed: it springs instead from a promise of mutual arousal, an eventuality that may elude two people who are naked and in bed together or, conversely, may take hold of another pair as they are ascending a mountainside in a chairlift, dressed in thick ski suits, mittens and woollen hats. While on screen the presenter praises a pistachio cornetto, back in the room the nakedness on the marital bed has some of the same sterile, affectless quality of a Baltic nudist beach.

The programme comes to an end, and Daisy sets aside her tools. Jim reaches across the bed, takes her hand and holds it lightly in his. Neither of them makes any further move. To a casual observer, the scene might look innocuous enough, but a significant event is in train: Jim is attempting to initiate sex.

Logic might suggest that being in a long-term relationship or being married must automatically guarantee an end to the anxiety that otherwise dogs attempts by one person to induce another to have sex. But while either kind of union may make sex a constant *theoretical* option, it will neither legitimate the act nor even ease the path towards it on any particular occasion. Moreover, against a background of permanent possibility, an unwillingness to have sex may be seen as constituting a far graver violation of the ground rules than a similar impasse might do in other contexts. Being turned down by someone we have just met in a bar is, after all, not so terribly surprising or wounding; there are methods for dealing with such a rebuff. Suffering sexual rejection by the person with whom we have pledged to share our life is a much odder and more humiliating experience.

It has now been a full four weeks since Daisy and Jim last made love. The entire country has emerged from winter during the intervening month. Bluebells have burst forth, new generations of robins have taken their first flights, bees have begun their tireless patrolling of the capital's flowerbeds. Long though this latest gap might seem, such lapses are not unusual for the couple: the one before stretched out to six weeks, and the one before that, five. When it comes to sex, Jim has developed a madman's memory for dates. In the whole of the previous year, he and his wife had intercourse only nine times.

For Jim, these statistics feel like a shameful reflection on some essential aspect of his self. In part, no doubt, it is a matter of injured pride, but it also has something to do with our larger culture – and, more specifically, with the extent to which recent history has placed a priority on the liberation of desire, on making sure that people no longer have to disguise their bodies in ill-fitting garments, or fear the prospect of raising unwanted children, or regard sex as being anything more or less than an emotionally enriching and innocent pastime.

It doesn't help that Jim feels unable to talk to anyone about the state of his and Daisy's sex life. Dinners with friends give him no opportunity to bring up a topic at once so serious and so inconsequential.

'You must be sleepy,' he now says to her, by which he means, 'I beg you to show me that you want me'.

'I had a really early start,' replies Daisy with a yawn – a statement that Jim's thirty-nine-year psychological history leads him to interpret as, 'I am thoroughly revolted by you.'

They shut off the lights and lie quietly side by side in the dark. Jim can hear and feel his wife turn over a few times before she finally finds a comfortable position, curled up with her back to him. There are noises outside – car horns, cats mewling, the occasional scream, the laughter of passers-by returning from an evening out – but within Jim, just the dull thud of his own misery.

2.

To begin with, and most innocently, the paucity of sex within established relationships typically has to do with the difficulty of shifting registers between the everyday and the erotic. The qualities demanded of us when we have sex stand in sharp opposition to those we employ in conducting the majority of our other, daily activities. Marriage tends to involve – if not immediately, then within a few years – the running of a household and the raising of children, tasks that often feel akin to the administration of a small business and that draw upon many of the same bureaucratic and procedural skills, including time management, self-discipline, the exercising of authority and the imposition of rules upon recalcitrant others.

Sex, with its contrary emphases on expansiveness, imagination, playfulness and a loss of control, must by its very nature interrupt this routine of regulation and self-restraint, threatening to leave us unfit or at the least uninclined to resume our administrative duties once our desire has run its course. We avoid sex not because it isn't fun but because its pleasures erode our subsequent capacity to endure the strenuous demands that our domestic arrangements place on us. Our repudiation of lovemaking may thus be likened to a mountain climber's or a runner's not wishing to luxuriate in the lyricism and hypnotic grandeur of a great poem, perhaps by Walt Whitman or Tennyson, just before scaling a peak or starting a marathon.

Sex also has a way of altering and unbalancing our relationship with our household co-manager. Its initiation requires one partner or the other to become vulnerable by revealing what may feel like humiliating sexual needs. We must shift from discussing practical projects – debating what sort of household appliance to acquire or where to go on holiday next year – to making the more challenging request that, for example, our spouse should turn over and take on the attitude of a submissive nurse, or put on a pair of boots and start calling us names. The satisfaction of our needs may force us to ask for things that are, from a distance, open to being judged both ridiculous and contemptible so that we may prefer, in the end, not to entrust them to someone on whom we must rely for so much else in the course of our ordinary, upstanding life.

The commonsense notion of love typically holds that a committed relationship is the ideal context in which to express ourselves sexually – the implication being that we won't have to be embarrassed by revealing some of our more offbeat needs to the person we have betrothed ourselves to for eternity, at an altar in front of 200 guests. But this is a woefully mistaken view of what makes us feel safe. We may in fact find it easier to put on a rubber mask or pretend to be a predatory, incestuous relative with someone we're not also going to have to eat breakfast with for the next three decades.

While the desire to split people into discrete categories of those we love and those we can have sex with may seem a peculiarly male phenomenon, women are far from innocent on this score themselves. The madonna/whore dichotomy has an exact analogy in the no-less-common nice-guy/bastard complex, wherein women recognize the theoretical appeal of warm, nurturing and communicative males but are at the same time unable to deny the superior sexual attraction of those cruel bandits who will take off for another continent the moment the lovemaking is finished. What unites the 'whore' and the 'bastard' in these two scenarios is their emotional and actual unavailability and therefore their power not to act as permanent witnesses to, and evocators of, our sexual vulnerability and strangeness. Sex may sometimes be just too private an activity to engage in with someone we know well and have to see all the time.

3.

Sigmund Freud went far beyond this. It was he who first, and most starkly, identified a much more complex and deep-seated reason for the difficulty many of us experience in having sex with our long-term partners. In an essay written in 1912 and bearing the awkwardly beautiful title 'On the Universal Tendency to Debasement in the Sphere of Love', Freud summed up the wrenching dilemma that seemed so often to afflict his patients: 'Where they love, they have no desire, and where they desire, they cannot love.'

By Freud's reckoning, our sex life will gradually be destroyed by two unavoidable facts connected to our upbringing: first, in childhood, we learn about love from people with whom taboo strictly forbids us to have sex; and second, as adults, we tend to choose lovers who in certain powerful (though unconscious) ways resemble those whom we loved most dearly when we were children. Together these influences set up a devilish conundrum whereby the more deeply we come to love someone outside of our family, the more strongly we will be reminded of the intimacy of our early familial bonds – and hence the less free we will instinctively feel to express our sexual desires with him or her. An incest taboo originally designed to limit the genetic dangers of inbreeding can thus succeed in inhibiting and eventually ruining our chances of enjoying intercourse with someone to whom we are not remotely related.

The likelihood of the incest taboo's re-emergence in a relationship with a spouse increases greatly after the arrival of a few children. Until then, reminders of the parental prototypes on which our choice of lovers is subconsciously based can be effectively kept at bay by the natural aphrodisiacs of youth, fashionable clothes, nightclubs, foreign holidays and alcohol. But all of these prophylactics tend to be left behind once the pram has been parked in the hall. We may remain ostensibly aware that we are not our partner's parent, and vice versa, yet this awareness will have a habit of becoming a more porous concept in both of our unconscious minds when we spend the greater part of every day acting in the roles of 'Mummy' and 'Daddy'. Even though we are not each other's intended audience for these performances, we must nevertheless be constant witnesses to them. Once the children have been put to bed, it may not be uncommon for one partner – in one of those slips of meaning Freud so enjoyed – to refer to the other as 'Mum' or 'Dad', a confusion that may be compounded by the use of the same sort of exasperated-disciplinarian tone that has served all day long to keep the young ones in line.

It can be hard for both parties to hold on to the obvious yet elusive truth that they are in fact each other's equals, and that however off-putting the thought of having sex with a parent may be, this is not really the danger they are facing.

4.

When men and women abandon long-established relationships to take up with new and younger lovers, their actions are often interpreted as being motivated by a simple and rather pathetic search for lost youth. The deeper, subconscious reason, however, may be far more poignant: those who leave may be endeavouring to escape the parental ghosts that seem to have subsumed their partners and, as a result, rendered impossible any sexual intimacy with them.

But when sex becomes mired in the incest taboo, the way out is not of course to begin all over again with a different partner, for fresh candidates will themselves end up morphing into parental figures, too, once the relationship has taken root. It is not a new person we require, but a new way of perceiving a familiar one.

How can we best go about effecting such a shift? One answer may be found in a sexual prac-tice that can only ever appeal to a small minority, but which nevertheless carries an underlying moral applicable to all long-term relationships.

There are some couples who take pleasure in together selecting a third person, a stranger, to have sex with one of them while the other watches. The voyeur willingly cedes his or her rightful position and derives erotic enjoyment from bearing witness to the induction of his or her spouse.

This is not an act of altruism. Rather, the new actor has been brought in for a particular purpose: to remind the voyeur of what is arousing about his or her partner. The voyeur uses the stranger's lust as a map to trace the way back to desires long obscured by the fog of routine. Through the agency of the stranger, the voyeur can feel the same excitement for a partner of twenty years as on the night they first met.

A variant on this approach involves one partner taking nude photographs of the other, posting them on a dedicated internet site, and then soliciting the frank comments of a worldwide audience.

Tradition, jealousy and fear are sufficiently strong to prevent such practices from ever catching on in a big way, but they show us with particular clarity certain mechanisms of perception that we would be wise to incorporate into all of our relationships. The solution to long-term sexual stagnation is to learn to see our lover as if we had never laid eyes on him or her before.

A less threatening and less dramatic version of this act of perception is readily available by checking in to a hotel room for a night. Our failure to notice the erotic side of our partner is often closely related to the unchanging environment in which we lead our daily lives. We can blame the stable presence of the carpet and the living-room chairs for our failure to have more sex, because our homes guide us to perceive others according to the attitude they normally exhibit in them. The physical backdrop becomes permanently coloured by the activities it hosts – vacuuming, bottle feeding, laundry hanging, the filling out of tax forms – and reflects the mood back at us, thereby subtly preventing us from evolving. The furniture insists that we can't change because it never does.

Hence the metaphysical importance of hotels. Their walls, beds, comfortably upholstered chairs, room-service menus, televisions and small, tightly wrapped soaps can do more than answer a taste for luxury; they can also encourage us to reconnect with our long-lost sexual

We cannot expect to be able to go on making love if the carpet is always the same. The Park Hyatt Hotel, Tokyo.

selves. There is no limit to what a shared dip in an alien bath tub may help us to achieve. We may make love joyfully again because we have rediscovered, behind the roles we are forced to play by our domestic circumstances, the sexual identities that first drew us together – an act of aesthetic perception that will have been critically assisted by a pair of towelling bathrobes, a complimentary fruit basket and a view out of a window onto an unfamiliar harbour.

5.

In further considering how we might manage to re-desire our spouse, we might find it instructive to look at the way in which artists approach the task of painting the world. While going about their quite different types of business, the lover and the artist nonetheless come up against a similar human foible: the universal tendency to become easily habituated and bored, and to declare that whatever is known is unworthy of interest. We are prone to long unfairly for novelty, kitschy romanticism, drama and glamour.

It lies in the power of certain great works of art, however, to induce us to revisit what we think we already understand and to reveal new, neglected or submerged enchantments beneath a familiar exterior. Before such works, we feel our appreciation of supposedly banal elements being reignited. The evening sky, a tree being blown by the wind on a summer day, a child sweeping a yard, or the atmosphere of a diner in a large American city at night are promptly revealed as not merely dull or obvious motifs but arenas of interest and complexity. An artist will find ways of foregrounding the most poignant, impressive and intriguing dimensions of a scene and fixing our attention on these, so that we will give up our previous scorn and start to see in our own surroundings a little of what Constable, Gainsborough, Vermeer and Hopper managed to find in theirs.

Aside from chefs, gourmands and farmers, few people in nineteenth-century France would have been likely to detect anything especially interesting in asparagus – that is, until Edouard Manet painted a tightly wrapped bunch in 1880 and thereby called attention to the inherent wonder of this spring vegetable's yearly apparition. However exemplary Manet's technical skills may have been, his painting achieves its stunning effect not by *inventing* the charms of asparagus but by *reminding* us of qualities that we knew

There are lessons for long-term relationships in the way that Manet approached asparagus. Edouard Manet, *Bunch of Asparagus*, 1880.

existed but that we have overlooked in our spoilt and habituated ways of seeing. Where we might have been prepared to recognize only dull white stalks, the artist observed and then reproduced vigour, colour and individuality, recasting his humble subject as an elevated and sacramental object through which we might access a redeeming philosophy of nature and rural life.

To rescue a long-term relationship from complacency and boredom, we might learn to effect on our spouse much the same imaginative transformation that Manet performed on his vegetables. We should try to locate the good and the beautiful beneath the layers of habit and routine. We may so often have seen our partner pushing a buggy, arguing with a toddler, crossly berating the electricity company and returning home defeated from the workplace that we have forgotten that dimension in him or her that remains adventurous, impetuous, cheeky, intelligent and, above all else, alive.

6.

Then again, if we have tried these solutions and they haven't worked, if sex with our long-term partner remains a rare and less-than-dynamic event, how justified should we be in feeling surprised, annoyed and bitter?

Modern society will be apt to give full credence to our frustration: anything less than complete satisfaction smacks of compromise and capitulation. Frequent and fulfilling sex with a long-term partner is viewed as the norm, and any falling away from it as pathology. The sex-therapy industry, developed primarily in the United States during the second half of the twentieth century, has focussed most of its efforts on assuring us that marriage should be enlivened by constant desire. It was the pioneers of sexology, William Masters and Virginia Johnson, who first articulated the bold view that it was every married person's ongoing right to enjoy good sex with his or her spouse, from the altar to the grave. In their bestselling *Human Sexual Inadequacy* (1970), they set out systematically to identify and provide antidotes for all the hurdles that a couple might face in their quest for this unending run of fulfilling sex: vaginismus, orgasmic dysfunction, dyspareunia, ejaculatory incompetence and the effects of aging.

Masters and Johnson equipped their book with helpful diagrams and kindly phrased suggestions

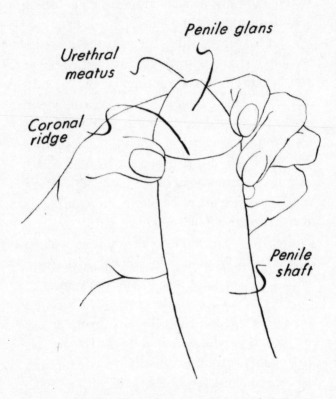

Expanding the frontiers of knowledge: a helpful illustration from Masters and Johnson's *Human Sexual Inadequacy*, 1970.

about helpful exercises that couples might avail themselves of. Read today, their sober prose is fearless and in its own way impressive, in its dedication to dragging into the light some of the quiet intensities of human suffering. For a problem as old as time, for instance, the authors offered a practical and deeply sympathetic approach:

> The first step in therapy for the incompetent ejaculator is for his wife to force ejaculation manually. It may take several days to accomplish this purpose. The important concept to project to both unit members is that there is no rush.

It is undoubtedly an evolution in civilization when such matters can be put into prose and discussed in an undramatic and unembarrassed way by two adults while their children are asleep downstairs.

Yet there is arguably also something peculiar, even perverse, in an attitude of mind that relentlessly pathologizes a failure to have regular sex. Might we not turn the issue on its head and suggest that far from being an indication that something is wrong, a gradual decline in the intensity and frequency of sex between a married couple is merely an inevitable fact of biological life and, as such, evidence of deep normality? To rebel against it is like protesting that we are not permanently happy. Given the rarity of good sex, is it really right that we should continue to regard frequency as the norm? It would of course be convenient if sex and marriage could peacefully coexist, but wishing does not make it so. Would there not therefore be a certain wisdom in redrawing our expectations, depathologizing and destigmatizing our so-called 'failures' and sometimes just turning over to the other side of the bed, ready to accept without rancour, with stoic calm, some of the necessary compromises of long-term love?

ii. Impotence

I.

It is generally easier to admit to having spent time in prison than to having suffered from impotence. There are few greater sources of shame for a man, or of feelings of rejection for his partner. It is a physical failure with moral connotations, flouting norms of decency and masculinity and seeming at once to rebuke the partner's personality and physical appearance. The tragedies that afflict the human race are many, but seldom are they as intense as those that strike in a bedroom after a couple have repeatedly tried and failed to secure the erection of the male. At such moments, suicide may no longer seem a remote or unreasonable possibility.

The real problem with impotence is less the actual loss of pleasure involved (which can be compensated for easily enough through masturbation) than the blow dealt to the self-esteem of both parties. Impotence is deemed a catastrophe because of an understanding of what flaccidity *means*.

Yet the argument that will be ventured here is that we are grievously mistaken in our methods of interpretation, for if we were to assess the matter more fairly, we would feel not only unembarrassed by occasions of psychologically created impotence, but perhaps even proud of them.

2.

We should start by sketching the broad outlines of a topic that deserves one day to be written up in the form of a serious scholarly monograph: the history of impotence.

Let us propose, though we have little concrete empirical evidence for the claim, that at the dawn of its existence mankind was rarely bothered by impotence. The early hominids who lived in clammy darkness in the caves of central France, or amid enervating heat in the straw huts of the Rift Valley, may have had a hard time finding food, evading dangerous animals, sewing underpants and communicating with faraway relatives, but having sex was a simple matter for them, because the one question that almost certainly never ran through the minds of male hunters as they lifted themselves up on their hirsute limbs was whether their partners were going to be in the mood that night – or whether they might instead feel revolted or bored by the sight of a penis, or just keen to spend a quiet evening tending to the fire. Reason and kindness had not yet intruded on the free flow of animal impulses – nor, in the West, would they do so convincingly for many millennia to come, until the influences of classical philosophy and Judeo–Christian ethics at last percolated through the general population in the centuries after the death of Christ. Impotence had its origins in the increase in empathy attendant on the promotion of the Golden Rule ('Do not do unto others as you would not have done unto you'); it was the strangely troublesome fruit of our new inclination to wonder what another might be feeling and then to identify with his or her potential objections to our invasive or unsatisfactory demands.

Accordingly, all but the least self-aware among us will sometimes be struck by how distasteful our desire for sex can seem to someone else, how contrary to reason it can appear, how peculiar and physically off-putting our flesh may be and how unwanted our caresses – and therefore how careful we ought to be in going about the business of seduction. The greater our power of imagination, the more acute and amplified will be our apprehension about giving offence – to the extent that even when sex is a legitimate possibility, our doubts may prove impossible to cast aside, with fatal consequences, if we are male, for our ability to maintain an erection. It is civilization itself, with its faith in human rights, its respect for kindness and its moral sophistication, which has unwittingly generated an inestimable increase in occasions of sexual fiasco. An advanced capacity for love and tenderness can ironically render us too sensitive to try to pester anyone else into having sex with us.

Civilization has surely brought with it virtues of enormous benefit to relationships between the genders, among them gentleness and tact, a spirit of equality and a greater fairness in the apportioning of domestic chores. We may have to admit, however, that it has also made it harder for us – or for *men*, at least – to have sex. We now know that we must never insist, never roughly thrust forward our needs and never regard another person as a mere instrument for our own use or pleasure.

Well-meaning though our hesitancy and embarrassment may be, and though based on the kindest of impulses, they risk cheating us of certain promising opportunities. Now and then we may cross paths with individuals who are not appalled by our longing for urgent and forceful sexual congress, and who see nothing disgusting in even the farthest erotic extremes. Yet these candidates may still require us to make the first move, perhaps because while they happen to want sex, they also need someone else to remind them of the fact. Their minds may be so busy with rational matters and daily distractions that only outside intervention can succeed in reacquainting them with their libidinous selves. If the deadlock of shyness is ever to be broken, one party must overcome the fear of displeasing the other and take a chance, gambling that in the end, perhaps after an interval of confusion and reluctance, sex will disclose its manifold attractions.

In its initial manoeuvres, therefore, the most loving, well intentioned and empathetic sex can sometimes look an awful lot like complete indifference to what someone else feels or wants.

3.

Impotence is at base, then, a symptom of respect, a fear of causing displeasure through the imposition of our own desires or the inability to satisfy our partner's needs. The popularity of pharmaceuticals designed to combat erectile dysfunction signals the collective longing of modern men for a reliable mechanism by which to override our subtle, delicate, civilized worry that we will disappoint or upset others.

A better and drug-free approach might consist in a public campaign to promote to both genders – perhaps via a series of billboards and full-page ads in glossy magazines – the notion that what is often termed 'nerves' in a man, far from being a problem, is in fact an asset that should be sought out and valued as evidence of an evolved type of kindness. The fear of being disgusting, absurd or a disappointment to someone else is a first sign of morality. Impotence is an achievement of the ethical imagination – so much so that in the future, we men might learn to act out episodes of the condition as a way of signalling our depth of spirit, just as today we furtively swallow Viagra tablets in the bathroom to prove the extent of our manliness.

iii. Resentment

I.

Let's return now to Daisy and Jim, our couple in South London who have not made love for a month. The reason Daisy doesn't want to have sex with her husband after they turn off the television and the lights is that she is furious with him, though this sentiment would come as quite a surprise to him – and indeed to her as well. She has seemed calm and measured all day. The two of them had a wholly polite, if somewhat superficial, supper together only a few hours earlier, during which she never complained or gave any other indication of distress. Furthermore, as she lies in bed, she herself has no inner awareness of having any active gripes against Jim. She isn't even thinking about him; she is feeling a bit sad, keen to be alone and rather worried about all the things she has to get done the next day.

The common conception of anger posits red faces, raised voices and slammed doors, but only too often it takes on a different form, for when it doesn't understand or acknowledge itself, it just curdles into numbness.

There are two reasons we tend to forget we are angry with our partner, and hence become anaesthetized, melancholic and unable to have sex with him or her. Firstly, because the specific incidents that anger us happen so quickly and so invisibly, in such fast-moving and chaotic settings (at breakfast time, before the school run, or during a conversation on mobile phones in a windy plaza at lunchtime) that we can't recognize the offence well enough to mount any sort of coherent protest against it. The arrow is fired, it wounds us, but we lack the resources or context to see how and where, exactly, it has pierced our armour. And second, we frequently don't articulate our anger even when we do understand it, because the things that offend us can seem so trivial, finicky or odd that they would sound ridiculous if spoken aloud. Even rehearsing them to ourselves can be embarrassing.

We may, for example, be deeply wounded when our partner fails to notice our new haircut or doesn't use a breadboard while cutting a bit of baguette, scattering crumbs everywhere, or goes straight upstairs to watch television without stopping to ask about our day. These hardly seem matters worth lodging formal complaints over.

To announce, 'I am angry with you because you cut the bread in the wrong way,' is to risk sounding at once immature and insane. An objection of this sort may indeed be both of those things, but given that immaturity and insanity by and large constitute the human condition, we would be well advised to stop subscribing to (and then suffering from), any more optimistic notions.

Comparable arguments, on topics objectively petty and absurd to outsiders, punctuate the history of every relationship. It comes down to ambition. To fall in love with another is to bless him or her with an idea of who he or she should be in our eyes; it is to attempt to incarnate perfection across a limitless range of activities, stretching from the highest questions (how to educate the children and what sort of house to buy) to the lowest (where the sofa should go and how to spend Tuesday evening). In love we are therefore never far from the possibility of a painful or irritating betrayal of one of our ideals. Once we are involved in a relationship, there is no longer any such thing as a minor detail.

Over the course of an average week, each partner in a couple may be hit by, and in turn fire, dozens of tiny arrows without even realizing it, with the only surface legacies of these wounds being a near-imperceptible cooling between them and, crucially, the disinclination of one or both to have sex with the other – for sex is a gift that is not easy to hand over once we are annoyed, especially when we aren't even aware we happen to be so.

The situation has a tendency to spiral into ever greater nastiness. The one who has done the unwitting hurting will be punished sexually, which will lead to the firing of yet more surreptitious arrows, causing wounds that themselves will be neither understood nor dealt with and will then inspire further covert acts of aggression and withholding.

Finally, the following sort of explosion is likely to occur, even between otherwise generous and rational people who are deemed to be reliable colleagues, loving friends and assets to their communities:

JIM: You don't want to have sex with me
    ever, do you?
DAISY: Yes, I do, but I'm not in the mood
    now.
JIM: You say that every single time.
DAISY: I do *not*. I just don't want to be
    forced.
JIM: I'm not trying to force you!

DAISY: You are, you're bullying me.

JIM: I'm starting to suspect you're frigid, you know.

DAISY: And I'm realizing you're rather nasty.

JIM: I'm going to sleep next door.

DAISY: Fine. I don't care in the least.

At any given moment, hundreds – perhaps thousands – of identical conversations are being had across the globe, often in its most privileged precincts, the sorts of places where there are no wars or desperate economic conditions, only well-stocked shops and expensive institutions of higher education. The waste of time and life seems appalling, for despite all the insults they may be trading, the combatants probably truly love each other and could be reciprocally kind, if only they could first work out how they managed to grow so angry.

2.

By this point in our history, as a species, we know full well why couples tear at each other and relationships collapse. The reasons are set forth in the sober pages of psychological hand-books bearing titles such as *Couples in Treatment: Techniques and Approaches for Effective Practice* (this particular volume is edited by two British psychotherapists, Gerald Weeks and Stephen Treat).

While the information is there for all to read, it has a cunning habit of being unavailable to us in moments of crisis. We lack objective onlookers to seek advice from and mantras to chant to stick good ideas in our minds. Our knowledge is intellectual and unrepeated. We are undone by the sheer speed with which disappointments occur and by our inability to pause and rerun the tape, to rise above the fray and shift the focus away from recrimination and towards an identification of the true sources of our hurt and fear.

In a more well-ordered world, rather than allow Jim and Daisy to press on any further in their attempts to quantify precisely how evil their partner allegedly is, Gerald Weeks and Stephen Treat would take charge of them, sit them down together in a quiet room and encourage them to retrace every step that led them to their private hell. In time and with effort, the couple might then begin to appreciate that their hostilities towards each other were shaped by the flow of their individual personalities through the distorting emotional canyons of their particular childhoods.

In a perfect world, all couples would be visited by a psychotherapist on a weekly basis, without even having to put themselves forward for the service. The session would simply be a regular feature of a good, ordinary life, as the Friday-evening meal is for Jews, and would offer some of the same cathartic function as this ritual. Above all, neither party would be made to feel by society that he or she was crazy for having therapy – which is currently the main reason people neglect to see therapists and therefore slowly go crazy.

This ideal therapist would take a history of a relationship, explore its current tensions and try to serve as a catalyst for the sort of change that the couple themselves were too weak, busy or confused to bring about on their own. She would remind her clients that every exchange, however minor, had meaning and could set off a chain of recriminations and resentments that would prevent them from wanting to have sex. She would teach them to treat the complicated business of being in a relationship with extraordinary care. She would ask them both to arrive at every session with a list of issues that had arisen during the previous week, and insist that they each listen to the other's complaints compassionately, without resorting to angry self-justification or injured self-pity. She would advise them that if they did not make love at least once a week, they would necessarily experience an excess of libido that might then seek other outlets, with consequent implications for their union. She would review their individual psychological histories and endeavour to help make the couple aware of some of the ways in which, because of their particular pasts, they might both be likely to distort or misread reality. And when arguments did flare up, she would urge each of them to see the other as being wounded and sad rather than malicious and spiteful.

This therapist would belong to a new kind of priesthood, designed for an age that no longer believes in religious forgiveness and understanding in the afterlife but that is still very much in need of those same qualities in the here and now.

3.

If such a service does not yet exist, it is only because capitalism is still in its infancy. We are able to have exotic fruit delivered to our doorsteps and construct micro-conductors, but we struggle to find effective ways of examining and healing our relationships. The problem is that we think we already know everything necessary about how to be with another person, without having bothered to learn anything at all. We are no more capable of figuring out how to handle this task on our own than we would be able intuitively to work out how to land a plane or perform brain surgery. Whereas most workplaces are now awash with artificial procedures designed to prevent employees from murdering one another, modern lovers still baulk at attempts to introduce standardized practices and external assistance into their relationships. The idea persists that too much *thinking* might make it impossible for us to *feel* – as if it weren't already quite plainly apparent that a large and constant amount of thinking may be the only thing that can keep us from destroying each other.

By overwhelming consensus, our culture locates the primary difficulty of relationships in finding the 'right' person rather than in knowing how to love a real – that is, a necessarily rather *unright* – human being. Our reluctance to work at love is bound up with our earliest experience of the emotion. We were first loved by people who kept secret from us the true extent of the work that went into it, who loved us but didn't ask us to return affection in a rounded way, who rarely revealed their own vulnerabilities, anxieties or needs and who were – to an extent, at least – on better behaviour as parents than they could be as lovers. They thereby created, albeit with the most benign of intentions, an illusion that has complicated consequences for us later on, insofar as it leaves us unprepared for the effort we must legitimately expend to make even a very decent adult relationship successful.

We can achieve a balanced view of adult love not by remembering what it felt like to be loved as a child but rather by imagining what it took for our parents to love us – namely, a great deal of work. Only through similar application will we be able to sort out which partner in our relationship is firing the arrows and why, and thereby stand a chance of enjoying a better union and, as a windfall, more frequent and more affectionate sex.

4. Pornography

i: Censorship

1.

When his demons grow unmasterable and Daisy is asleep, Jim often surreptitiously gets out of bed and climbs the stairs to visit the computer in the small study on the floor above.

As its defenders are forever pointing out, the internet is a superlative educational tool, connecting the intermittent intelligences of the continents' scattered populations into a single, gigantic and ceaselessly active global mind. With just a few clicks and taps on the keyboard, Jim can find himself navigating the virtual stacks of the Library of Congress, checking the weather in southern Italy, looking at classic cars at a show in California or investigating contrasting graphs of the planet's median air temperatures over the past two decades.

Yet with equal ease, he can of course run a search on 'slutty teenagers fucking' and lose his mind. No wonder sales of serious literature are down across the world: books are going to have to be really interesting to compete with this. Anything else – a spacecraft's landing on Mars, a child's first nativity play, the discovery of fifteen previously unknown Shakespeare folios – will struggle. The real question of the age is why a man might ever choose to lead his own life rather than just click on, obsessively, from Amateurs to Blondes, Bondage to Interracial, Outdoors to Redheads and Shemales to Voyeur.

2.

Pornography is often accused (typically by those blessed souls whose entire direct experience of the subject comprises a peek or two inside an old issue of *Playboy* and perhaps an abbreviated preview of the adult channel, glimpsed some years ago on a hotel television set) of being comfortingly 'fake' and therefore unthreatening to the conduct of any sensible and intelligent existence. But this is unfortunately far from the truth. Modern pornography now looks so real

as to resemble our own lives in every detail –
with the significant difference, of course, that
in the former everyone happens to be having
continuous, beatific sex.

The associated waste of time is naturally
horrific. Financial analysts put the value of the
online pornography industry at $10 billion a year,
but this figure doesn't begin to evoke its true cost
in terms of squandered human energy: perhaps
as many as two hundred million man-hours
annually that might otherwise have been devoted
to starting companies, raising children, curing
cancer, writing masterpieces or sorting out the
attic, are instead spent ogling the mesmerizing
pages of sites such as www.hotincest.com and
www.spanksgalore.com.

3.

How deeply contrary pornography is to the rest
of our plans and inclinations becomes clear only
after orgasm. Where just a moment before we
might have sacrificed our worldly goods for one
more click, now we must confront with horror
and shame the temporary abandonment of our
sanity. Nobility as Aristotle conceived of it in

the *Nicomachean Ethics* – 'the full flourishing of what is most distinctive human in accordance with the virtues' – has surely been left far behind when an anonymous woman somewhere in the former Soviet Union is forced onto a bed, three penises are roughly inserted into her orifices and the ensuing scene is recorded for the entertainment of an international audience of maniacs. We are far from dignity, happiness and morality – but also not so far, in certain eyes at least, from pleasure.

Yet this poison is not easy to resist. An unlikely and partly unwitting alliance between Cisco, Dell, Oracle and Microsoft on the one hand and thousands of pornographic-content providers on the other has exploited a design flaw of the male gender. A mind originally designed to cope with little more sexually tempting than the occasional sight of a tribeswoman across the savannah is rendered helpless when bombarded by continual invitations to participate in erotic scenarios far exceeding any dreamt up by the diseased mind of the Marquis de Sade. There is nothing robust enough in our psychological makeup to compensate for developments in our technological capacities, nothing to arrest our passionate desire to renounce all other priorities for the sake of a few more minutes (which might turn out to be four hours) in the darker recesses of www.spring-breakdelight.com.

It was not so difficult to concentrate on reading Chekhov's short stories by candlelight when the only other diversion on offer was a chat with a neighbour who lived a twenty-minute walk away down the lane. But what chance do Chekhov or any other writers stand when we can split our Dell screen into two, on the left side arrange a photo collage of naked cheerleaders, and on the right, with the help of MSN Messenger, conduct a real-time conversation with a svelte twenty-five-year-old pole dancer (in reality a doughy male truck driver of 53) who will gently encourage us, in our own guise as a curious but uninitiated teenage lesbian, to take the first tentative steps towards our sexual awakening?

4.

When the intellectual framework behind our modern secular societies was first developed, by such seventeenth- and eighteenth-century thinkers as John Locke, Voltaire, Thomas Jefferson and Thomas Paine, the ideal of personal liberty was set at its centre. In their 'good society', citizens would be left alone to read what they wished, look at whatever images they liked and worship any god they chose. The only limits to be imposed on the individual's freedom were those justified by a need to prevent harm to others: people would not be permitted to bludgeon their neighbours to death or rob one another of their livelihoods, but short of such extreme behaviours, they would be allowed to do as they pleased. This fundamental principle was famously asserted in John Stuart Mill's essay *On Liberty* (1859): 'The only freedom which deserves the name, is that of pursuing our own good in our own way, so long as we do not attempt to deprive others of theirs, or impede their efforts to obtain it. Each is the proper guardian of his own health, whether bodily, or mental and spiritual.'

Even today, when we meditate on what is most distinctive and honourable about contemporary democracies, we will tend to single out freedom. Our automatic defence of this ideal rests on two foundations. First, our embrace is cautionary: we are well aware of the dangers associated with any sort of state intervention. Believing it impossible for one person really to know how another should live, we hold that the potential benefits to be derived from curtailing others' activities are far outweighed by the inherent perils. It seems preferable to leave people to work out their salvation in their own ways, rather than run the risk of causing a catastrophe by interfering. Lest any doubt should persist on this score, the spectres of Hitler and Stalin are routinely invoked as reminders of what can happen when one person decides he knows what is best for everyone else.

Second, and more optimistically, our defence of freedom rests on the belief that we human beings are at heart mature, rational creatures, able to adequately assess our own needs, look after our own interests and get along perfectly well by ourselves, without requiring a great deal of protection. What we are exposed to doesn't need monitoring, for we don't tend to be overly influenced by things we look at or read about. We aren't going to be irreparably harmed by a book or a picture; we aren't likely to become violent after reading a bloodthirsty novel or lose our moral bearing on account of seeing a film or a photograph. Our mental equilibrium is stronger than that. We aren't made of blotting paper; we can safely live with, and take pride in, a free press and a democracy of ideas.

5.

In almost every detail, these secular tenets contradict the beliefs of most religions – unsurprisingly, perhaps, given that the philosophy of modern liberalism evolved largely in reaction to the drift of religious doctrine. For their part, the faiths have always argued that they are in possession of some highly reliable understandings of right and wrong and hence are morally obligated to impose their value systems, if necessary with vigour and coercion. They have also held that humans are not at all impervious to the messages they find around them. They may be deeply affected by material they read or look at, and so must constantly be protected from themselves. They stand in need of censorship.

The very word is normally terrifying, evoking the Soviet and Nazi experiments as well as the vengeful stupidities of the Catholic Inquisition. Yet before we reject the idea of censorship out of hand, even though we are on a slippery slope at the bottom of which lie some appalling scenarios, it may be worth entertaining the possibility that there could be such a thing as a beneficial and necessary variety of censorship. Perhaps we really are, as many religions would have it, vulnerable to what we read and see; perhaps the influence of books and visual materials *doesn't* just wash over us. Because we are passionate and largely unreasonable, buffeted by destructive hormones and desires, it doesn't take much to make us lose sight of our long-term ambitions. Although this permeability may insult our self-image, the wrong pictures may send us down a fatal track; unhelpful reading material may deflect the needle of our ethical compass; and a few ill-intentioned adverts in a glossy magazine can (as advertisers well know) play havoc with our values. In such cases, a bit of censorship might not be such a bad idea. Without, of course, ceding all of our freedoms to an arbitrary and tyrannical authority, we ought nevertheless, sometimes and in some contexts, to be willing to accept a theoretical limit to some of our rights, if only for the sake of our own well-being and our capacity to flourish. In moments of lucidity, we should be able to see for ourselves that untrammelled liberty can paradoxically trap us, and that – when it comes to internet pornography, for instance – we might be doing ourselves a favour if we willingly consented to cede certain of our privileges to a benign supervisory entity.

It is perhaps only those people whose logical selves have never been obliterated by the full force of sex who can remain uncensorious and liberally 'modern' on the subject. Philosophies of sexual liberation seem to appeal largely to those who harbour no especially destructive or weird desires which they long to satisfy once they have been liberated.

By contrast, anyone who has experienced the power of sex in general, and of internet pornography in particular, to reroute rational priorities, is unlikely to be quite so sanguine on the topic of sexual freedom. After sufficient late-night hours spent obsessively watching a succession of people undress and penetrate one another, even the most libertarian among us might find themselves calling for someone to make a giant bonfire out of every last server, router, data-farm and cable on the planet, so as to put a definitive end to the system responsible for delivering a diet of poison into our homes and minds.

Pornography, like alcohol and drugs, undermines our ability to endure certain kinds of suffering which we have to experience if we are to direct our lives properly. More specifically, it reduces our capacity to tolerate our ambiguous moods of free-floating worry and boredom. Our feelings of anxiety are genuine but confused signals that something is amiss, and so need to be listened to and patiently interpreted – processes which are unlikely to be completed when we have to hand, in the computer, one of the most powerful tools of distraction ever invented. The entire internet is in a sense pornographic, a deliverer of a constant excitement that we have no innate capacity to resist, a seducer that leads us down paths that for the most part do nothing to answer our real needs. Furthermore, the ready availability of pornography lessens our tolerance for the kind of boredom that grants our mind the space it needs to spawn good ideas – the creative sort of boredom we may luxuriate in during a bath or on a long train journey. Whenever we feel an all but irresistible desire to flee from our own thoughts, we can be quite sure there is something important trying to make its way into our consciousness – and yet it is precisely at such pregnant moments that internet pornography is most apt to exert its maddening pull, assisting our escape from ourselves and thereby helping us to destroy our present and our future.

6.

Only religions still take sex seriously, in the sense of properly respecting its power to turn us away from our priorities. Only religions see it as something potentially dangerous and needing to be guarded against. We may not sympathize with what they would wish us to think about in the place of sex, and we may not like the way they go about trying to censor it, but we can surely – though perhaps only after killing many hours online at www.youporn.com – appreciate that on this one point religions have got it right: sex and sexual images can overwhelm our higher rational faculties with depressing ease.

Given its resistance to censorship and its faith in mankind's maturity, the secular world reserves a special scorn for Islam's promotion of the hijab and the burka. The idea that women should have to cover themselves up from head to toe so as not to distract male believers' focus from Allah seems preposterous to the guardians of secularism. Would a rational adult man really turn his life upside down because he caught a glimpse of a pair of beguiling female knees or elbows? And who but a mental weakling could be seriously affected by the spectacle of a group of half-naked teenage girls sauntering provocatively down the beachfront?

Secular societies have no problems with bikinis or sexual provocation because, among other things, they do not believe that sexuality and beauty have such extraordinary power over people. Men are presumed to be entirely capable of watching a group of young women cavort, whether online or in the flesh, and then getting on with their lives as though nothing out of the ordinary had just happened.

Religions are often mocked for being prudish, but insofar as they warn us against sex, they do so out of an active awareness of the charms and the power of desire. They wouldn't judge sex to be quite so bad if they didn't also understand that it could be rather wonderful. The problem is that this wonderful thing can get in the way of some other important and precious concerns of ours, such as God and life.

We may not want to go so far as to veil beauty, but perhaps we can come to see the point of censoring the internet and applaud any government attempts to reduce the ready and unchecked flow of pornography down our fibre-optic cables. Even if we no longer believe in a deity, we may have to concede that a degree of repression is necessary

It is only religions that still take seriously the power of sex to rearrange our priorities.

both for the mental health of our species and for the adequate functioning of a decently ordered and loving society. A portion of our libido has to be forced underground for our own good; repression is not just for Catholics, Muslims and the Victorians, but for all of us and for eternity. Because we have to go to work, commit ourselves to relationships, care for our children and explore our own minds, we cannot allow our sexual urges to express themselves without limit, online or otherwise; left to run free, they destroy us.

ii. A New Kind of Porn

I.

Then again, the real problem with pornography may be not its widespread availability but its nature and quality. It would not cause us so many difficulties if it weren't quite so far removed from all the other concerns that a reasonably sensible, moral, kind and ambitious person might have – sex aside. However, as currently constituted, pornography asks that we leave behind our ethics, our aesthetic sense and our intelligence when we contemplate it, in order that we give ourselves over wholly to the most mindless sort of lust. The plots are daft, the lines of dialogue absurd, the actors exploited, the interiors ugly and the photographs voyeuristic – hence the feeling of disgust that overtakes us the moment we are done with it.

Yet it is possible to conceive of a version of pornography that wouldn't force us to make such a stark choice between sex and virtue – a pornography in which sexual desire would be invited to support, rather than permitted to undermine, our higher values. In fact, something not dissimilar to this already exists, and in what may seem the single most unlikely place imaginable: the sphere of Christian art.

During a certain few periods in its history, Christian art understood that sexual desire did not necessarily have to be the enemy of goodness, and could even, if properly marshalled, lend energy and intensity to it. In altarpieces by Fra Filippo Lippi or Sandro Botticelli, not only is the Madonna beautifully dressed and set against an enchanting background, she is also good-looking – indeed, in many cases, indisputably sexy. Although this point is not typically dwelt upon in art-historical discussions or museum catalogues, the Mother of Christ can quite often be an unambiguous turn-on.

In deliberately striving for this effect, Christian artists were not contravening the caution generally shown by their religion towards sexuality; rather, they were affirming that at selected moments, sexuality could be invited to promote a project of edification. If viewers were to be persuaded that Mary had been one of the noblest human beings who ever lived – the embodiment of kindness, self-sacrifice, sweetness and goodness – it might help if she was also pictured as having been, in the most subliminal and delicate of ways, rather alluring sexually.

Sexiness lending support to, rather than undermining, our interest in kindness and virtue. Sandro Botticelli, *The Madonna of the Book*, c.1483.

The advantage of having sexual fantasies while looking at a Botticelli Madonna rather than at a stereotypical product of the modern porn industry is that the former doesn't compel us to make an uncomfortable choice between our sexuality and other qualities we aspire towards. It allows us to give free rein to our physical impulses while remaining aesthetically sensitive and morally aware. It gives us a chance, in short, to bridge the gap between sex and virtue.

These paradigmatic images of Mary hint at what an enlightened or integrated pornography of the future might look like. Ideally, it would excite our lust in contexts that also presented other, elevated sides of human nature – in which people were being witty, for instance, or showing kindness, or working hard or being clever – so that our sexual excitement could bleed into, and enhance our respect for, these other elements of a good life. No longer would sexuality have to be lumped together with stupidity, brutishness, earnestness and exploitation; it could instead be harnessed to what is noblest in us.

2.

This new kind of pornography would have the incalculable benefit of mitigating some of the self-hatred that the current genre tends to produce once we have finished with it. Adolescent boys, a demographic obsessed with pornography in a way that much concerns their own consciences as well as upsetting their parents, would be absolved of having to choose between loving to look at sexy pictures and caring about their family, schoolwork and sporting achievements. The new pornography would combine sexual excitement with an interest in other human ideals. The usual animalistic categories and hackneyed plots, replete with stock characters seemingly incapable of coherent speech, would give way to pornographic images and scenarios based around such qualities as intelligence (showing people reading or wandering the stacks in libraries), kindness (people performing oral sex on one another with an air of sweetness and regard) or humility (people caught looking embarrassed, shy or self-conscious). No longer would we have to make a painful choice between being human and being sexual.

The pornography of the future: we could be interested in sex *and* intelligence.
Becky in the Den, Jessica Todd Harper, 2003.

5. Adultery

i. The Pleasures of Adultery

I.

We are unlikely to be able to get a grip on this notorious subject if we don't first allow ourselves to acknowledge just how tempting and exhilarating adultery can be, especially after a few years of marriage and a couple of children. Before we can begin to call it 'wrong', we have to concede that it is also very often – for a time, at least – profoundly thrilling.

So let us imagine yet another scenario. Our man, Jim, is in his office, interviewing candidates for a freelance graphic-design job. He has already spent a few hours meeting with a succession of young, goatee-bearded men when the final prospect arrives. Named Rachel, she's twenty-five (Jim is almost forty, and feeling very aware of death) and is wearing a pair of jeans, trainers and a dark-green V-neck jumper over nothing much else, calling attention to her androgynous upper body. They talk of printing costs, margins, paper weights and fonts – but of course, Jim's thoughts are elsewhere. We would have to fear for the state of mind of the man who did *not* respond to this picture of youth, health and energy.

There is in Rachel none of the sullenness of the supermodel, none of the resentment towards their own good looks that beauty sometimes generates in ambitious and intelligent young women, and which causes them to take offence at just how much more interested most of the world is in their physique than in their ideas. Instead she has the guileless, innocent enthusiasm of someone brought up by two loving, elderly parents on a remote farm and who has never watched television or been to secondary school.

To describe what Jim wants as 'sex' is severely to foreshorten the roots of his excitement. The old English synonym for the noun is unusually apt in this case, for in essence Rachel is provoking in Jim a longing to *know* her – know her thighs and ankles and neck, naturally, but also her wardrobe, the titles of the books she has on her shelf, the smell of her hair after a shower, the nature of her character when she was a little girl and the confidences she exchanges with her friends.

In this instance, as in woefully few others in Jim's life, fate takes an unusual turn. Several months after Rachel's project with his firm is finished, he is asked to go on an overnight trip to Bristol, to attend an awards ceremony with one of his clients at a Holiday Inn off the M4 – and discovers in the lime-green foyer at the start of the evening that Rachel happens to be there too. She has forgotten him entirely, but after a few clues she is customarily effusive and rapidly agrees to his suggestion that they meet up in the bar after the ceremony. Like a first-time murderer who intuitively knows how to distribute stones in a body bag, Jim sends an email to Daisy, wishing her and their two children good night and warning that he may not have a chance to call her later – as he usually does in the circumstances – because the evening threatens to drag on.

They have a glass of wine together in the otherwise deserted bar around midnight. Jim's flirtation is precise and to the point. The boldness displayed by middle-aged married men when they are trying to seduce other women should never be confused with confidence: it is just the fear of death, which breeds an awareness of just how infrequently they are ever going to have the opportunity to sample such moments again. It is this that gives Jim the energy to press on in ways he never would have dared to do when he was young and single, when life seemed like a limitless expanse stretching out before him and he could still afford the luxury of feeling shy and self-conscious.

Their first kiss takes place in the corridor leading to the lifts. He presses her up against the wall, next to a poster advertising a discounted rate for a family stay with a free brunch for the kids on Sunday. Her tongue greets his eagerly; her body pushes rhythmically up against his. This quickly enters the pantheon of the greatest moments of Jim's life.

2.

After he returns home from Bristol, everything continues as it was. He and Daisy put the children to bed, go out for supper, discuss their need for a new oven, quarrel and have as little sex as before.

Of course, Jim lies about the whole thing. We live in moralistic times. Our age allows most things to happen before marriage but accepts

nothing much thereafter. The newspapers pub-
lish a rolling succession of stories about the sexual
indiscretions of footballers and politicians, and
readers' comments on these reflect the kind of
response that Jim's activity could be expected to
provoke from most fellow citizens. He would be
branded a cheat, a scumbag, a dog and a rat.

These labels terrify Jim, but at the same time,
part of him wonders why he should have to submit to such easy moralism. We might follow him
in his scepticism. Let's take the view, for a moment,
that what happened between Jim and Rachel was
not especially wrong. For that matter, let's go even
further and venture that (contrary to all public
verdicts on adultery), the real fault might consist
in the obverse – that is, in the *lack* of any wish
whatsoever to stray. This might be considered
not only weird but *wrong* in the deepest sense of
the word, because irrational and against nature.
A blanket refusal to entertain adulterous possi-
bilities would seem to represent a colossal failure
of the imagination, a spoilt imperturbability in
the face of the tragically brief span we have been
allotted on this earth, a heedless disregard for the
glorious fleshly reality of our bodies, a denial of
the power that should rightly be wielded over our
more rational selves by such erotic triggers as

the flirtatious enlacing of fingers under a conference table during a meeting and the surreptitious pressing-together of knees at the end of a restaurant meal, by high-heeled shoes and crisp blue shirts, by grey cotton underwear and Lycra shorts, by smooth thighs and muscular calves – each a sensory high point as worthy of reverence as the tiles of the Alhambra or Bach's Mass in B minor. Wouldn't the rejection of these temptations be itself tantamount to a sort of betrayal? Would it really be possible to trust anyone who never showed any interest at all in being unfaithful?

3.

Society holds that married people who discover that their spouses are having affairs have every right to be furious with them and throw them out of the house, cut up their clothes and massacre their reputations in front of their friends. Adultery is seen as providing ample grounds for the cheated-upon party to feel incensed and outraged, as well as abundant cause for the cheating party to apologize in extreme ways for his or her horrid actions.

But here again, might we not suggest that

however hurt the betrayed party may feel, fury at the news of the other's infidelity is not entirely warranted. The fact that the straying spouse has had the temerity to imagine, let alone act on the idea that it might be of interest to push a hand inside an unfamiliar skirt or pair of trousers should not truly come as such a surprise after a decade or more of marriage. Should there really be a need to apologize for a desire that could hardly be more understandable or ordinary?

Rather than ask their 'betrayers' to say they are sorry, the 'betrayed' might begin by saying sorry themselves – sorry for *being* themselves, sorry for getting old, sorry for being boring sometimes, sorry for forcing their partners to lie by setting the bar of truthfulness forbiddingly high and (while we are at it), sorry for being human. It can too easily seem as if the adulterous spouse has done everything wrong, and the sexually pure one nothing. But this is an abbreviated understanding of what 'wrong' entails. Certainly adultery grabs the headlines, but there are lesser, though no less powerful, ways to betray a partner, including not talking to him or her enough, seeming distracted, being ill-tempered or simply failing to evolve and enchant.

4.

A spouse who gets angry at having been betrayed is evading a basic, tragic truth: that no one can be everything to another person. Rather than accept this horrific thought with dignified grace and melancholy, 'betrayed' spouses are often encouraged to accuse their 'betrayers' of being morally in the wrong for finding fault with them. However, the real fault in the situation lies in the ethos of modern marriage, with its insane ambitions and its insistence that one person can plausibly hope to embody the eternal sexual and emotional solution to another's every need.

Taking a step back, what distinguishes modern marriage from its historical precedents is its fundamental tenet that all our desires for love, sex and family ought to reside *in the selfsame person*. No other society has been so stringent or so hopeful about the institution of marriage, nor ultimately, as a consequence, so disappointed in it.

In the past, these three very distinct needs – for love, sex and family – were wisely differentiated and separated out from one another. The troubadours of twelfth-century Provence, for example, were experts in romantic love. They were well versed in the ache inspired by the sight of a graceful figure, in the anxious sleeplessness suffered at the prospect of a meeting and in the power of a few words or a glance to invoke an elevated state of mind. But these courtiers expressed no wish to link such prized and deeply felt emotions to parallel, practical intentions – no wish, that is, to raise a family, or even have sex, with those they so ardently loved.

The libertines of early-eighteenth-century Paris were just as devoted, but in their case to sex rather than romance: they worshiped the delight of unbuttoning a lover's garments for the first time, the excitement of exploring and being explored by another at leisure by candlelight, the subversive thrill of seducing someone covertly during Mass. But these erotic adventurers also understood that such pleasures had very little to do with either love or the rearing of a nurseryful of children.

For its part, the impulse to raise a family has been well known to the largest share of humanity since our earliest upright days in East Africa. In all this time, however, it seems to have occurred to almost no one (until very recently, evolutionarily speaking) that this project might need to be fused together with constant sexual desire as well as frequent sensations of romantic longing at the sight of a fellow parent across the breakfast table.

The independence, if not the incompatibility, of our romantic, sexual and familial sides was held to be an untroubling and universal fact of life until the mid-eighteenth century, when, among the members of one particular segment of society in the more prosperous countries of Europe, a remarkable new ideal began to take shape. This ideal proposed that henceforth, spouses ought not to be satisfied with just tolerating each other for the sake of their children; instead, and in addition, they were to regard it as their due to deeply love and desire each other. Their relationships were to wed the romantic energy of the troubadours to the sexual enthusiasm of the libertines. Thus was set before the world the compelling notion that our most pressing needs might be solved all at once, *with the help of only one other person.*

It was no coincidence that the new ideal of marriage was created and backed almost exclusively by a specific economic class: the bourgeoisie, whose balance of freedom and constraint it also uncannily mirrored. In an economy expanding rapidly thanks to technological and commercial developments, this newly emboldened class no longer needed to accept the restricted expectations of the lower orders. With a little extra money to spare for relaxation, bourgeois lawyers and merchants could now raise their sights and hope to find in a partner more than merely someone who could help them to survive the next winter. However, their resources were not unlimited. They didn't have the boundless leisure of the troubadours, whose inherited wealth had ensured that they could, without difficulty, spend three weeks writing a letter in celebration of a beloved's brow. The bourgeoisie had businesses to run and storehouses to manage. Nor could they permit themselves the social arrogance of the aristocratic libertines, whose power and status had bred in them a confident nonchalance about breaking others' hearts and shattering their own families, and given them the means to mop up any unpleasant messes that their antics might leave behind.

The bourgeoisie was hence neither so downtrodden as not to have time for the luxury of romantic love nor so liberated from necessity as to be able to pursue erotic and emotional entanglements without limit. The idea of achieving fulfilment through an investment in a single, legally and eternally contracted partner was a fragile answer to their particular balance of emotional need and practical constraint.

The bourgeois ideal rendered taboo a host of faults and behaviours that previously would have been, if not completely ignored, then at least not seen as automatic cause for ending a marriage or breaking up a family. A barely tepid friendship between spouses, adultery, impotence – all of these now took on a new and grave significance. The notion of entering into a loveless or indifferent marriage was as much anathema to a bourgeois as the concept of *not* having outside affairs would have been to a libertine.

The progress of bourgeois romantic ambition can be usefully traced through fiction. Jane Austen's novels still feel recognizably modern to us because her aspirations for her characters mirror, and helped to create, the ones we have for ourselves. Like Elizabeth Bennet in *Pride and Prejudice* and Fanny Price in *Mansfield Park*, we long to reconcile our wish for a secure family with a sincerity of feeling for our spouse. But the history of the novel also points to darker aspects of the romantic ideal. *Madame Bovary* and *Anna Karenina*, arguably the two greatest novels of the European nineteenth century, confront us with a pair of heroines who, in accordance with their eras and social positions, long for a complex set of qualities in their partners: they want them to be at once husbands, troubadours and libertines. In both cases, however, life gives them only the first of the three. Emma and Anna are caged within economically secure yet loveless marriages that in earlier ages might have been a source of envy and celebration, but which now seem intolerable. At the same time, they inhabit a bourgeois world that cannot countenance their attempts to conduct extramarital affairs. Their eventual suicides illustrate the irreconcilable nature of this new model of love.

5.

The bourgeois ideal is not entirely an illusion. There are some few marriages that perfectly fuse together the three golden strands of fulfilment – romantic, erotic and familial – and which will never be troubled by adultery. We cannot say, as cynics are sometimes tempted to do, that happy marriage is a myth. It is infinitely more tantalizing than that: it is a possibility, yet a very, very rare one. There is no metaphysical reason why marriage should not honour all our hopes; the odds are just stacked overwhelmingly against us – a tragic truth we should calmly face head on, before life drives it home to us in its own brutal way, and at a time of its choosing.

ii. *The Stupidity of Adultery*

I.

But let's flip the coin once more: if seeing marriage as the perfect answer to all our hopes for love, sex and family is naive and misguided, so too is believing that adultery can be an effective antidote to the disappointments of marriage.

What is ultimately 'wrong' with the idea of adultery, as with a certain idea of marriage, is its idealism. While it may look at first sight like a cynical and unhopeful activity to engage in, adultery in fact suggests a conviction that we might somehow magically rearrange the shortcomings of our marriage through an adventure on the side. Yet to credit this notion is to misunderstand the conditions life imposes on us. It is impossible to sleep with someone *outside* of marriage and not spoil the things we care about *inside* it – just as it is impossible to remain faithful in a marriage and not miss out on some of life's greatest and most important sensory pleasures along the way.

2.

There is no answer to the tensions of marriage, if what we mean by an 'answer' is a settlement in which no party suffers a loss, and in which every positive element that we care about can coexist with every other, without either causing or sustaining damage.

The three things we want in this sphere – love, sex and family – each affects and harms the others in devilish ways. Loving a person may inhibit our ability to have sex with him or her. Having a secret tryst with someone we don't love but do find attractive can endanger our relationship with the spouse we love but are no longer turned on by. Having children can imperil both love and sex, and yet neglecting the kids in order to focus on our marriage or our sexual thrills may threaten the health and mental stability of the next generation.

Periodically, frustration breeds an impulse to seek a utopian solution to this mess. Perhaps an open marriage would work, we think. Or a policy of secrets. Or a renegotiation of our contract on a yearly basis. Or more childcare. All such strategies are fated to fail, however, for the simple reason that loss is written into the rules of the situation. If we sleep around, we will put at risk our spouse's love and the psychological health of our children. If we don't sleep around, we will go stale and miss out on the excitement of new relationships. If we keep an affair secret, it will corrode us inside and stunt our capacity to receive another's love. If we confess to infidelity, our partner will panic and never get over our sexual adventures (even if they meant nothing to us). If we focus all of our energies on our children, they will eventually abandon us to pursue their own lives, leaving us wretched and lonely. But if we ignore our children in favour of our own romantic pursuits as a couple, we will scar them and earn their unending resentment. Marriage is thus a bit like a bed sheet that can never be straightened: when we seek to perfect or ameliorate one side of it, we may succeed only in further wrinkling and disturbing the others.

3.

What more realistic mindset, then, might we take with us into a marriage? What kinds of vows might we need to exchange with our partner in order to stand a sincere chance of mutual fidelity? Certainly something far more cautionary and downbeat than the usual platitudes would be in order – for example: 'I promise to be disappointed by you and you alone. I promise to make *you* the sole repository of my regrets, rather than to distribute them widely through multiple affairs and a life of sexual Don Juanism. I have surveyed the different options for unhappiness, and it is you I have chosen to commit myself to.' These are the sorts of generously pessimistic and kindly unromantic promises that couples should make to each other at the altar.

Thereafter, an affair would be a betrayal only of a reciprocal pledge to be disappointed in a particular way, not of an unrealistic hope. Spouses who had been cheated upon would no longer furiously complain that they had expected their partner to be happy with them per se. Instead they could more poignantly and justly cry, 'I was relying on you to be loyal to the specific variety of disappointment that I represent.'

4.

When the idea of a love-based marriage took hold in the eighteenth century, it replaced an older and more prosaic rationale for betrothal, whereby couples got married because they had both reached the proper age, found they could stand the sight of each other, were keen not to offend both sets of parents and their neighbours, had a few assets to protect and wished to raise a family.

The bourgeoisie's new philosophy, by contrast, legitimated only one reason for marriage: deep love. This condition was understood to comprise a variety of hazy but totemic sensations and sentiments, including the lovers' being unable to bear being out of each other's sight, their each being physically aroused by the other's appearance, their being certain that their minds were in perfect tune with each other, their wanting to read poetry to each other by moonlight and their desiring to fuse their souls together into one.

In other words, marriage shifted from being an *institution* to being the *consecration of a feeling*, from being an externally sanctioned rite of passage to being an internally motivated response to an emotional state.

Justifying the shift in the eyes of its modern defenders was a newly intense dread of what was known as 'inauthenticity', a psychological phenomenon whereby a person's inner feelings differed from those expected of him or her by the outer world. What the old school would have respectfully called 'putting on a show' was now recategorized as 'lying', while 'faking things to be polite' was more melodramatically recast as 'betraying oneself'. This emphasis on achieving congruence between inner and outer selves required strict new qualifications about what a decent marriage would have to entail. To feel only intermittent affection for a spouse, to have mediocre sex six times a year, to keep a marriage going for the wellbeing of the children – such compromises were considered abdications of any claim to be fully human.

5.

As young adults, most of us start out by feeling an intuitive respect for the idea of a love-based marriage. We can hardly avoid this reverence, given our cultural bias towards it, and yet as we get older, we will usually begin to wonder whether the whole thing might not be just a fantasy dreamt up by a group of adolescent-minded authors and poets a few hundred years ago – and whether we mightn't be better off under an older, institution-based system that served humanity well enough for most of its history theretofore.

Such a re-evaluation may be prompted by an awareness of how chaotic and misleading our feelings can be. We may, for example, see an attractive face at a street crossing and want to turn our life upside down as a result. When a tempting person with whom we have been having an erotic exchange in an internet chat room suggests a meeting at an airport hotel, we may be tempted to blow up our life in favour of a few hours' pleasure. There are times when we feel sufficiently angry with our spouse that we would be happy to see him or her knocked down by a car; but ten minutes later, we may be reminded that we would die rather than go on alone. During the longueurs of weekends, we may be desperate for our children to grow up, lose their interest in trampolining and leave us alone for ever so that we can read a magazine for once, and enjoy a tidy living room – and then a day later, at the office, we may want to howl with grief because a meeting looks like it's going to overrun and we realize we'll miss out on putting them to bed.

The defenders of feeling-based marriage venerate emotions for their sincerity and authenticity, but they are able to do so only because they avoid looking too closely at what actually floats through most people's emotional kaleidoscopes in any given period: all the contradictory, sentimental and hormonal forces that pull us in a hundred often crazed and inconclusive directions. To honour every one of our emotions would be to annul any chance of leading a coherent life. We could not be fulfilled if we weren't inauthentic some of the time, perhaps even a lot of it – inauthentic, that is, in relation to such things as our passing desires to throttle our children, poison our spouse or end our marriage over a dispute about changing a light bulb.

Romanticism highlighted the perils of inauthenticity, but we will face no fewer dangers if we attempt always to bring our outer life into line with our inner one. It is giving our feelings too great a weight to want them to be lodestars by which the major projects of our lives may be guided. We are chaotic chemical propositions, in dire need of basic principles that we can adhere to during our brief rational spells. We should feel grateful for, and protected by, the knowledge that our external circumstances are often out of line with what we feel; it is a sign that we are probably on the right course.

6.

We can welcome marriage as an institution that
endures from day to day without seeming to pay
too much mind to what its members are feeling.
Such benign neglect may in fact better reflect
the individuals' long-term wishes than a system
that would hourly take their emotional pulse and
adjust their status accordingly.

Marriage happens also to suit children well.
It spares them anxiety over the consequences
of their parents' arguments: they can feel confident that their mum and dad like each other well
enough to work things out, even though they may
bicker and fight every day, as kids themselves do
in the playground.

In a well-judged marriage, spouses should
not blame each other for occasional infidelities;
instead they should feel proud that they have for
the most part managed to remain committed to
their union. Too many people start off in relationships by putting the moral emphasis in the
wrong place, smugly mocking the urge to stray
as if it were something disgusting and unthink-
able. But in truth, it is the ability to stay that is
both wondrous and worthy of honour, though it
is too often simply taken for granted and deemed

the normal state of affairs. That a couple should be willing to watch their lives go by from within the cage of marriage, without acting on outside sexual impulses, is a miracle of civilization and kindness for which they ought both to feel grateful on a daily basis.

Spouses who remain faithful to each other should recognize the scale of the sacrifice they are making for their love and for their children, and should feel proud of their valour. There is nothing normal or particularly pleasant about sexual renunciation. Fidelity deserves to be considered an achievement and constantly praised – ideally with some medals and the sounding of a public gong – rather than discounted as an unremarkable norm whose undermining by an affair should provoke spousal rage. A loyal marriage ought at all times to retain within it an awareness of the immense forbearance and generosity that the two parties are mutually showing in managing not to sleep around (and, for that matter, in refraining from killing each other). If one partner should happen to slip, the other might forgo fury in favour of a certain bemused amazement at the stretches of fidelity and calm that the two of them have otherwise succeeded in maintaining against such great odds.

IV. Conclusion

1.

We might be so much better off if we didn't have a sex drive; for most of our lives, it causes us nothing but trouble and distress. In its name, we do revolting things with people we don't really like, only to feel disgusting and sinful afterwards. Those we desire usually dismiss us for being too ugly or not their type; the cute ones have always already got a boyfriend or a girlfriend; most of our early adult life is a continuous round of rejection, sad music and bad pornography. It seems a miracle when eventually someone takes pity on us and gives us a chance, yet even then, we find ourselves before long starting to take an interest in other people's legs and hair again. We would be so nice without sex – nice in the way that seven-year-old boys and girls are, full of sweetness and wonder about the lives of marmosets or deer. As we age, we can look forward to the horror and

humiliation of not being able to perform, of looking lustfully at the wrists and ankles of people
who turn out to have still been babies when we
were already at university and of having to watch
the slow collapse of our own once fresh and
elastic body. On a bad day, the entire enterprise
appears designed to defeat us.

2.

But there is of course another side to it, one of
ecstasy and discovery. Perhaps the best time to
get a sense of this is on a clear evening in a large
city in the summer, at around six-thirty, when the
workday is largely over and the streets smell of
diesel, coffee, fried food, hot tarmac and sex. The
pavement swarms with people in suits, cotton
print dresses and loose-fitting jeans. Already the
lights on the bridges have come on, and airplanes
are pirouetting above; all the sensible folk have
headed back home to the suburbs for their children's bathtime, but for those who are staying, the
night promises warmth, intrigue and mischief.

Sex gets us out of the house and out of ourselves. In its name, we stretch out our horizons
and intermingle unguardedly with random mem-

bers of our species. People who otherwise keep themselves to themselves, who tacitly believe they have nothing much in common with the ordinary mass of humanity, enter bars and discos, climb nervously up tenement stairs, wait in unknown precincts, shout to make themselves heard over the throb of the music and talk politely with respectable mothers in living rooms adorned with ornaments and school-prize photos, while upstairs the mothers' grown-up children change into new pairs of trim grey underwear.

In the name of sex, we expand our interests and our reference points. To fit in with our lovers, we become fascinated by the details of eighteenth-century Swedish furniture, we learn about long-distance cycle riding, we discover South Korean moon jars. For sex, a burly yet tender tattooed carpenter will sit in a cafe opposite an elfin PhD student with a fringe, half listening to her tortuous explanation of the meaning of the Greek word *eudaimonia* and letting his eyes trace patterns across her flawless porcelain skin as someone grills sausages in the background.

There would be so much less to do without sex. No one would bother to open jewellery stores, embroider lace, serve food on silver platters or hoist hotel rooms onto pontoons over tropical lagoons. The greater part of our economy would be meaningless without sex as a driving force or an organizing principle. The mad energy of the trading floors, the padded gold-leaf dressing rooms of Dior on Bond Street, the gatherings at the Museum of Modern Art, the black cod served at rooftop Japanese restaurants – what are all these for if not to help along the sort of processes whereby two people will eventually end up making love in a darkened room while sirens wail in the street below?

Only through the prism of sex does the past become properly intelligible. The apparent foreignness of ancient Rome or Ming Dynasty China cannot in the end have been so great, whatever the barriers of language and culture, because there, too, people felt the pull of flushed cheeks and of well-formed ankles. During the reign of Moctezuma I in Mexico or that of Ptolemy II of Egypt, it would have felt more or less the same to enter into or be entered by someone and to gasp at the pressure of her body or his against ours.

Without sex, we would be dangerously invulnerable. We might believe we were not ridiculous. We wouldn't know rejection and humiliation so intimately. We could age respectably, get used to our privileges and think we understood what was going on. We might disappear into numbers and words alone. It is sex that creates a necessary havoc in the ordinary hierarchies of power, status, money and intelligence. The professor will get on her knees and beg to be flogged by an unschooled farmhand. The CEO will lose his reason over an intern; it will seem of no consequence that while he commands a few million, she rents a basement room. His only priority will be her pleasure. For her he will learn the names of bands he has never heard of before, he will go into a shop and buy her a lemon-yellow dress that won't fit her, he will be kind where he has always been dismissive, he will acknowledge his folly and his humanity and when it is all over, he will sit in his expensive German car outside his pristine family home and weep without measure.

We might even embrace the pain sex causes us, for without it we wouldn't know art and music quite so well. There would be so much less point to Schubert's Lieder or Natalie Merchant's *Ophelia*, to Bergman's *Scenes from a Marriage* or Nabokov's *Lolita*. We would be so much less well acquainted with agony, and therefore so much crueller and less ready to laugh at ourselves. When every contemptuous but fair thing has been said about our infernal sexual desires, we can still celebrate them for not allowing us to forget for more than a few days at a time what is really involved in living an embodied, chemical and largely insane human life.

Homework

A large number of books, articles, films and conversations contributed towards the ideas in this book. The following were useful.

I. Introduction

Pessimism about human nature, sex included, is beautifully explored by Pascal in his *Pensées*, by Arthur Schopenhauer in his *Maxims on the Wisdom of Life* and by John Gray in his *Straw Dogs*. All three authors are alive to the thought that cheering someone up should never be confused with telling him or her something cheerful. As they recognize, it is far better to say extreme and grim things that will lead to the redrawing of expectations, and thereby occasion gratitude for small mercies.

II. The Pleasures of Sex

There is a surprising amount to be learnt about our fantasies from Nancy Friday's *My Secret Garden* and Shere Hite's *The Hite Report*. Friday's chapters on incest, prostitution and rape are particularly compelling.

Fetishes are amply documented and taxonomized by Richard von Krafft-Ebing in *Psychopathia Sexualis* and by Havelock Ellis in his *Studies in the Psychology of Sex*. Both books are, unfortunately, very boring.

David Perrett's *In Your Face: The New Science of Human Attraction* provides a good introduction to the evolutionary–biological perspective on beauty and sex. Kenneth Clark's *The Nude* is impressive on themes of beauty and desire. For Ingres, Andrew Carrington Shelton's monograph, *Ingres and his Critics*, is a useful source.

Wilhelm Worringer's *Abstraction and Empathy* puts forward his thought-provoking theory on the psychology of artistic taste.

The significance of beauty and its connection to virtue and morality are exquisitely explored by John Armstrong in *The Secret Power of Beauty*.

The best film ever made about fetishism is Eric Rohmer's *Le genou de Claire*.

There is more about Natalie Portman at www.natalieportman.com and more on Scarlett Johansson at www.scarlettjohansson.org.

The Italian fashion label Marni, at www.marni.com, makes some of the best flat shoes on the planet.

III. The Problems of Sex

The difficulties we face with sex in long-term relationships are among the topics considered in a collection of essays called *Rethinking Marriage*, edited by the psychoanalyst Christopher Clulow. Freud is also interesting at many points, especially in his *Three Essays on the Theory of Sexuality*.

William Masters and Virginia Johnson are fascinating in their *Human Sexual Inadequacy*, which feels, in the reading, almost like a novel about twentieth-century America masquerading as a guide on how to overcome premature ejaculation, impotence and vaginismus.

Couples seeking to reinvigorate their relationships should contemplate a stay at a branch of the Park Hyatt hotel chain: www.park.hyatt.com. Predictably and sadly, this will be ruinously expensive.

There is more on Manet and asparagus in *Manet, inventeur du moderne* by Stéphane Guégan and John Lee.

I have learnt about pornography from www.pornhub.com. There are some good insights to be had into censorship and the Catholic justification for it in Henry Kamen's *The Spanish Inquisition*. Cécile Laborde discusses the hijab in *Critical Republicanism: The Hijab Controversy and Political Philosophy*.

What a pornography of the future might look like is hinted at in some of the superlative images in Jessica Todd Harper's book, *Interior Exposure*.

Marriage and adultery are covered in Tony Tanner's classic study, *Adultery and the Novel*. John Armstrong is again strong on this theme in *Conditions of Love* – as is Gustave Flaubert, of course, in *Madame Bovary*. For my part, I haven't changed my mind about some of the things I wrote about in my first book, *Essays in Love*.

Overall, the whole theme of love and marriage is best captured by Ingmar Bergman in his film *Scenes from a Marriage,* which all prospective spouses should be forced to watch by government decree before they tie the knot.

IV. Conclusion

The sweaty charms of sexuality are best experienced in Manhattan in late July. Natalie
Merchant's album *Ophelia* is an outstanding
choice for anyone who has just been left in love.
Arthur Schopenhauer (see notes on the Introduction) isn't bad either.

Photographic Credits

The author and publisher would like to thank the following for permission to reproduce the images used in this book:

Kama Sutra. Album painting, India, late 18th c. / early 19th c. Private Collection. Photo: Werner Forman

Masaccio, *Adam and Eve Banished from Paradise*, c.1427. The Brancacci Chapel, Santa Maria del Carmine, Florence. Photo: The Bridgeman Art Library

Aeroplane toilet © Rex Features

Gentleman's wristwatch, 1940s, by Vacherin Constantin of Geneva

Ladies' Baffin loafer, 2011, by Bertie Shoes

Comparison of two female faces. Plate III, Figure G from *In Your Face: The New Science of Human Attraction*, 2010, by David Perrett. Reproduced by permission of the author

Comparison of two male faces, ibid., p.81, figure
4.5

Jean-Auguste-Dominique Ingres, *Madame
Antonia Devaucay de Nittis*, 1807. Musée
Condé, Chantilly. Photo: The Bridgeman Art
Library

Green silk printed dress by Marni Edition

Pink and black silk pussybow blouse by D&G
Dolce & Gabbana

Scarlett Johansson © Rex Features

Natalie Portman © Getty Images

Facade of the Church of Santa Prisca y San
Sebastian, Taxco © Mone Rosales / Fotolia

Agnes Martin, *Friendship*, 1963. Incised gold leaf
and gesso on canvas. Fractional and promised
gift of Celeste and Armand P. Bartos, MoMA,
New York © 2011. Agnes Martin/DACS,
London. Photo: Scala, Florence

Caravaggio, *Judith Beheading Holofernes*, 1599.
Palazzo Barberini, Rome. Photo: The
Bridgeman Art Library

Luxury room at the Park Hyatt Hotel, Tokyo.
Photo: courtesy Park Hyatt, Tokyo

Edouard Manet, *A Bunch of Asparagus*, 1880. Wallraf-
Richartz-Museum, Cologne. Photo: Erich
Lessing/akg-images

Explore the Other 'Maintenance Manuals for the Mind' in The School of Life Library

How to Think More About Sex
Alain de Botton
ISBN 978-1-250-03065-8

How to Stay Sane
Philippa Perry
ISBN 978-1-250-03063-4

How to Find Fulfilling Work
Roman Krznaric
ISBN 978-1-250-03069-6

How to Change the World
John-Paul Flintoff
ISBN 978-1-250-03067-2